DESIGNING GARDENS
WITH PLANT SHAPES

DESIGNING GARDENS WITH PLANT SHAPES

CAROL J. SMITH

THE CROWOOD PRESS

First published in 2011 by
The Crowood Press Ltd
Ramsbury, Marlborough
Wiltshire SN8 2HR

www.crowood.com

British Library Cataloguing-in-Publication Data
A catalogue record for this book is available from the British Library.

ISBN 978 1 84797 279 8

Frontispiece
White garden delphiniums. (Photo: Rhoda Nottridge)

Dedication
To Lily Mia, my granddaughter, born 19 November, 2010

Acknowledgements
I would like to thank everyone, from the planting of the seed for *Designing Gardens with
Plant Shapes*, to the final mature specimen. Firstly Colin, my wonderful husband and best
friend, whose encouragement, patience, and belief in me as both garden designer and
writer, spurred me on, in times of feeling absolutely sapped. My son Kevin, for his
interest and caring, even while he was cycling from Cambridge to Morocco! My daughter
Sharon, a constant source of inspiration, taught me all my computer skills, and has
provided an IT specialist back up service like no other! My mum: my gardening buddy
and the inspiration for so much of my plant knowledge. My father John and his partner
Marie-Therese, who have encouraged me to follow my path and passion – in particular
my passion for this book. My dear friends – Sue Evans, Tina Williams, Diane Elt, Joy
Beech, Elaine Normoyle, Sonya and Pete Hartwell, and Sharon Davies – have all been
brilliant sounding boards for my ideas, and have encouraged and inspired me. Lecturers
and ex-colleagues at Pershore College and latterly University of Gloucester – particularly
Chris Beardshaw, Simon Rose, Duncan Coombes, Tony Davy, John Edgeley, Steve Box,
Phil Oakley, David Booth and Richard Sneesby; thank you all for your support and
encouragement during my student days, and later as a lecturer and designer, and in taking
the plant shapes idea through to a book.

Typeset by Jean Cussons Typesetting, Diss, Norfolk

Printed and bound in Singapore by Craft Print International Ltd

CONTENTS

INTRODUCTION

There is no doubt that a well planned and executed planting scheme has more chance of success than one that has been developed without a plan; purely because every aspect of the required planting has been considered and carefully thought through. Time spent on planning the scheme allows for research and ultimate choice of the correct plants for the given growing environment. Options are explored by the designer in order to come up with the scheme best suited to both the client brief and existing growing conditions.

The options are many and varied, some more obvious than others, such as the use of colour combinations and harmonies, the provision of seasonal interest and succession planting. Other options which provide a more subtle element could be scent or variety and contrast of leaf form and texture; a fine example of this is the small evergreen *Sarcococca confusa* with its glossy, highly reflective leaves in complete contrast to the large, grey and furred, almost strokeable, leaves of *Verbascum olympican*. There is a vast variety of choices available, so it is of no surprise that many garden design students, newly qualified garden designers and amateur gardeners are at a loss to know where to begin.

The traditional method of drafting a planting scheme is to compile a plant list as the first stage. This assumes that the student/designer has the required knowledge base of plant names in order to achieve this. Of course this is not always the case; this is the most difficult knowledge to acquire, due to the names being in Latin. The naming system, known as *Nomenclature*, is hundreds of years old and was invented by Linnaeus.

Using the traditional method, plants are chosen according to their suitability to the given growing environment and, of course, their individual characteristics, such as eventual height, width and season of interest. This choosing process relies heavily upon the gardener's knowledge base; if not, then a time-consuming research process is the only way to determine that the plant choices are correct and appropriate. This is the process by which a gardener not only selects plants, but also, over a period of time, gradually increases and develops their own plant knowledge; coupled with hands-on experience in plant use and the observation of how those plants fail or thrive.

A small percentage of failure is acceptable, and can be due to a variety of factors, other than 'wrong plant, wrong place'. However, this scenario is one that we would wish to avoid; it is imperative to the long-term success of the planting scheme that the gardener has worked through a process that eliminates, as far as is possible, any element that might cause plants to fail.

Developing in parallel with the technical data base is the gradual acquisition of a visual memory of what particular plants look like; for example, if I were to ask you to think of a plant that is very familiar and commonly seen, such as a daisy, the majority of people would see a picture of a daisy in their mind's eye – this is our 'visual' reference book, and again something that is acquired and developed over an extended period of time, the length of which is variable, according to how much exposure the individual has to plants.

Taking all of this into consideration, we can see

OPPOSITE: **Spring bulbs. (Photo: Rhoda Nottridge)**

why learning the skills and knowledge required, to reach the point of being fully equipped to design a planting scheme can be such a long, exhausting process, and how the application of the acquired knowledge base plays such a primary role in the process.

In general, there are two categories of 'planting designers': those who choose to study the whole subject in more depth and embark on a formal education course, and those keen gardeners who learn more by experience – naturally there are overlaps between these two groups. However, there is also a gap between these two groups in terms of available methods. This 'gap' can be filled by the Plant Shapes Method described in this book.

THE PLANT SHAPES METHOD

The Plant Shapes Method avoids the dreaded 'writer's block' syndrome, or more appropriately 'planting design block'. The Plant Shapes Method is a quick, easy method to begin planning a planting scheme, whether faced with a small area, a whole garden with which the gardener is not satisfied or a completely new garden.

To start designing a planting scheme, the method employs some basic drawing of the nine plant shapes; followed by a succession of steps that add further 'visual' information. A pictorial form of the planting scheme is developed, without having to open a book or rely on a technical knowledge base. Initially, it sidesteps all the 'head stuff' and takes the gardener straight into the 'visual' aspects of how the scheme will look.

It is a creative process, using basic drawing skills, which, when the drawing is completed, provides the designer with a considerable amount of 'plant requirement' criteria, upon which the research for the appropriate plants can be based. The plant research, therefore, is not just the final stage; but also commences from an informed starting point. This is preferable to sitting at a desk surrounded by books, experiencing a sense of bafflement and inadequacy, and learning by expensive mistakes when plants fail. The Plant Shapes Method makes the early years of planting

design a much more enjoyable and creative process.

There is another side to this, which especially applies to the working garden designer, and that is the issue of time, and how long is allocated for the drafting of the planting plan. This is an issue that affects, in particular, qualified garden designers working to a project time scale, and students working to an assignment hand-in date. For them, the Plant Shapes Method considerably reduces the amount of 'thinking time' and enables them to reach the point of producing a drawing representative of the scheme in a considerably reduced time frame.

The 'time' issue does not apply to the amateur gardener in the same way. For them, the method provides a practical, hands-on, visual approach, by which the planting scheme can be designed and represented. In the absence of a 'plant name' knowledge base, the scheme could be taken to a reputable garden centre and professional advice sought, regarding the appropriate plants to fulfil the criteria. This 'visual' of the proposed planting scheme is an invaluable tool for demonstrating the proposed scheme.

The aim of the method is to instil a sense of confidence and empowerment to the user, whether artistic or not, whether a gardener, designer or student. The more the method is used, the more confidence levels increase; to the point where, in the case of the garden designer in particular, by using very quick sketches the method can be used to both explore and demonstrate a variety of planting scheme options, and to demonstrate the overall impact that the chosen scheme will have on the developing garden.

The method is best suited for use on smaller areas, but if a larger planting area is to be designed, then, by dividing the area into a series of smaller sections, and using a simple labelling system, for example A-B, C-D, and so forth, larger-scale design can be made more manageable.

The first part of this book provides the reader with an in-depth understanding of the various theoretical aspects underlying planting design. This provides a firm foundation for the second part of the book, which comprises drawn examples of the nine plant shapes, and a selection of plants appropriate to each shape. The reader is guided through a series of practical drawing exercises using the plant shapes, with further plant requirements being added as either colour or text or both, the end result of which is a fully annotated, three-dimensional drawing of a planting scheme, complete with all of the information needed to commence researching and choosing plants.

Chapter 8 has detailed drawings of examples of planting design schemes that will be valuable as a source of reference and inspiration. The book concludes with a structured planting project process, detailing the role of the designer within this process, which will help the gardener organizing a new planting scheme.

This book has come about after many years of working with plants in my own gardens, in nurseries, as a garden designer, and while teaching Planting Design and Identification to students with a broad range of skills and plant knowledge base. It became clear that there was a need for a method of planting design that was more creative in its initial stages, and therefore would enable the gardener to pick up their pencil and get started. A magazine article written some four years ago by Ruth Chivers in *Gardening Which?* magazine talked about plant shapes and used them to infill and improve a problem border – this is what inspired me to develop the Plant Shapes Method as a series of practical lectures. This is a complete process with which to design a planting scheme. Due to its simplicity, anybody who reads this book will be able to design their own planting scheme, whether for personal use, a college assignment or a client. There is nothing more satisfying than planning a planting scheme and seeing it come into reality.

1 THE THEORY OF PLANTING DESIGN

A naturally occurring planting that demonstrates the effectiveness of using a limited palette of plants in large drifts.

In this chapter we shall be looking at the nine planting design principles, the organic element in planting (the characteristics, horticultural requirements, basic considerations, density of plants and general maintenance) and the designer/graphic style.

WHAT IS PLANTING DESIGN AND WHAT IS ITS PURPOSE?

Most of us have a garden, which is usually a selection of plants, a lawn and some form of hard landscaping that may be of our choosing or may be inherited. Either way, there is a need for the garden to be cared for and maintained; if it is not maintained, plants have a habit of returning to nature and the whole thing looks somewhat wild and unkempt. That may be fine for some, but the majority of people want to enjoy their gardens, and take great pleasure in choosing plants, mowing the lawn and planning what the garden is going to look like. Many people visit garden centres to purchase plants and, it has to be said, are often disappointed with the results, either because the plants fail to thrive or because they simply do not look right when planted in their final destination. This is the point at which the advice is sought either of a professional gardener

Dark purple iris with orange geum.

to assist with general maintenance; or of a garden designer, whose job it is to maximize and develop the potential of the garden to become a beautiful space that the client/owner can enjoy.

Planting design helps us to make the best use of an existing garden or to plan a new planting scheme. Planting design is a subject full of unfamiliar terminology and concepts, which introduces the learner, whether student, designer or keen gardener, to a very different way of looking at a garden and its plants. Most people who are interested in or studying gardening and design initially think of plants purely from a 'horticultural needs' perspective, such as what soil the plant likes, or whether it prefers full sun or shade. These are the two of the commonest and most familiar growing requirements of a plant, and the framework within which planting schemes are appraised.

However, the process of producing a successful planting scheme is rather more complex than simply fulfilling the growing requirements of plants. Planting design encourages us to apply 'seen', but commonly not defined, phenomena as a set of 'rules' that can be easily followed. Once the principles of planting design have been introduced and understood, it is as if a door opens on to a world of perceiving and observing plants through completely new eyes. Plants are so much more than just their growing requirements; they have characteristics and personalities of their own and, like human individuals, are much more than just their physical bodies.

An example will help to demystify this concept. The cordyline is an evergreen Mediterranean plant that likes free-draining soil and plenty of sun. That, very simply, describes the growing requirements of the cordyline. If we now look at the cordyline and describe its individual characteristics, we see that it has a spiky, architectural shape almost like a firework exploding, which is very dramatic, and quite modern-looking. These are the qualities that the cordyline will bring to the planting scheme. This is one of the fundamental – and fascinating – skills of planting design: to develop the ability to see how the plant appears to you and describe it in your head, because this is how it will perform when planted. And once you, as designer or gardener start to observe plants in this way, you really get to know them from a completely different perspective. Plants never appear the same again.

In order to gain further understanding of the term 'planting design' we need to define what it is that makes a particular planting scheme successful. Here I need to mention that planting design, like art, is a very subjective matter. What is beautiful to look at for one designer/gardener may not be attractive to another. A good example of this is the work of the gardener/designer Christopher Hamilton Lloyd (1921–2006), whose death was a great loss to the horticultural world. As well as writing a number of books on gardening, his life was spent developing a wonderful garden at Great Dixter, along with his head gardener and great friend Fergus Garrett. Christopher Lloyd was a consummate plantsman and loved nothing more than to experiment with his plantings; his experiments with colour use often caused shock and surprise to plant lovers and garden visitors. He would think nothing of planting a vibrant lilac *Erysimum* 'Bowles Mauve' alongside bright orange tulips – and as you can see from this photo of a similar pairing, it worked!

Thus because of the subjective nature of planting design, it is difficult to define the constituents of a successful planting scheme. Where do we start? Is it a standard of horticultural perfection, whereby we have a collection of perfectly formed, unblemished plants? Or is it the way that the plants have been used? Both of these things will play their part in our reaction to the planting, and whatever our particular gardening interests, we all react in a positive or negative fashion to planting.

We need some sort of criteria or framework by which a planting scheme can be both planned and assessed. These criteria, namely 'planting design principles', are the foundations upon which planting design rests. Thousands of years ago, the first three design principles were defined by Marcus Vitruvius Pollio (c.80–70BC– c.15BC). Over time, the number of design principles has increased in order to fulfil the need for

a framework within which to describe and define aspects of design – in this case, planting design. Of course, opinions will vary from one person to another; however, by working within a framework we at least have a common language with which to assess, observe and plan planting schemes. Planting design principles act as guidelines against which planting schemes, whether proposed or existing, can be both assessed and planned. Understanding and knowing these principles will clearly help with planting design, however small or large the scheme. Broadly speaking, there are eight planting design principles:

- Form
- Rhythm
- Focal point
- Harmony
- Contrast
- Texture
- Balance
- Unity

In the next section we shall look at each of these principles in turn.

Trees planted with small gaps to create a fast rhythm.

Trees planted with longer gaps to create a slow rhythm.

PLANTING DESIGN PRINCIPLES

Form

This refers to both the overall plant shape and to evergreen plants, which together provide permanent 'form' throughout the year. Excellent examples of evergreens with very distinctive shapes can be seen in the conifer family. Certain deciduous trees, even though they lose their leaves in the autumn, can also provide a skeletal type of 'form' through the winter months by their overall outline shape and the branch formation within it. For example, hornbeam (*Carpinus betulus*) and oak (*Quercus*) are classic examples of trees that, even with bare branches, are easily recognizable.

Plant shapes, the commonest 'forms', are described in Chapter 5, with examples of plants for each shape. Form can also be introduced into a planting scheme by using clipped evergreens (topiary); commonly seen examples of this are balls and spirals of box (*Buxus*) and standard bay (*Laurus*) trees.

Rhythm

Rhythm is achieved by the consideration of spacing in-between plants, usually of the same variety. Because the plant type is repeated, the eye singles out and follows the repeated shape or colour; an avenue or line of trees, for example, is usually defined by low level planting in both height and interest, or no planting at all below the tree line. However, there is always an exception to the rule, and rhythm can also be created in a scheme by the repetition of a certain colour placed at regular intervals. Rhythm is created by the speed at which the eye moves from plant to plant or tree to tree. The closer the plants are together, the more the rhythm is increased; the further the plants are apart, the more it is slowed down. Picture in your mind's eye a tree-lined avenue: as you look from tree to tree, a rhythm is created due to the equal spacing between the trees. Above and left are photos that demonstrate both a fast and a slow rhythm.

Focal point

This refers to the positioning of a plant in such a way that it acts as a central point of interest within a planting scheme or garden, almost like the conductor of an orchestra. A focal point within a planting scheme or border can be achieved by choosing a plant that has, for

Cedrus atlantica glauca positioned to act as a focal point.

Colours in harmony.

example, an unusual growth habit or a strong form, or displays beautiful flowers at a particular season. For example, the magnolia tree is frequently seen as a focal point plant in the spring, when there is very little else in flower to compete with it. Conversely, if we think about autumn foliage colour, many examples spring to mind of plants that display fantastic, bright orange foliage in the autumn. Plants can also be used as a singular focal point by positioning them at the end of a vista, perhaps planted in a highly ornate pot raised up from the ground.

Harmony

If a planting scheme is to be generally pleasing, it needs to have a dominant tone and colour that runs through all the plants in varying degrees; this gives all the plants something in common, a link that creates visual harmony. So by choosing colours from the same range (blues harmonizing with lilacs, yellows harmonizing with oranges, and so on) we can ensure that the planting is pleasing to look at. Harmony can also be ach-ieved by using plant shapes that blend together, support each other, and bring out each other's best qualities. This will be demonstrated in Chapter 5.

In a planting scheme that uses harmonizing colours the plants appear as one, because no one colour dominates the others. Harmonizing colours can be from any part of the spectrum, as long as they are in the same range. They are relax-ing and soothing to look at, perhaps because the brain only has to interpret one 'set' of colours. It is well known that reds are regarded as hot, stim-ulating colours and blues are regarded as cool, calming colours; interestingly, however, a 'hot border', that is, a border containing only red plants, may be vibrant and exciting and energiz-ing, but it is still relaxing in a way, because the eye and brain are only having to interpret one colour. We shall look at the effects of colour in more detail in Chapter 7.

The contrast of *Eschscholzia* and blue *Salvia*.

Contrast

Contrast, when applied to plants, is for the most part achieved by the use of colours deliberately chosen to contrast with each other and therefore command visual attention. Contrast can also be brought into a planting scheme by using a variety of very different plant shapes, such as, for exam-ple, a tall columnar yew (*Taxus baccata*) planted with a clipped sphere of box. These two very strong shapes will compete for dominance and also have contrasting colours that will be more rapidly recognized by the eye. This creates high drama within a planting scheme and the eye cannot help but be drawn to contrasting colours.

Strongly contrasting colours – almost a clash.

The large, grey-felt leaves of *Stachys Byzantina*.

harder to interpret what is being seen. Somehow there is a disjointed feel and a sense of unrest to this type of scheme, as the plants and colours jostle for dominance.

Texture

Plant foliage is the biggest provider of texture. A classic example is *Stachys byzantina*, otherwise known as 'Rabbits Ears', which is almost exactly what the large, soft, grey, furry leaves look like; they make you want to stroke them! In contrast, there are the large, smooth, green and glossy leaves of the hosta family.

The strongest effect of smooth glossy leaves is that they reflect light and therefore act almost as a mirror to bounce light around. Over the years, many varieties of hosta have been bred with variegation ranging from very bright whites to creamy yellows. This is why the hosta is a very popular plant choice for use in shade. Not only does it tolerate low light levels, it thrives in them and increases the 'light effect' in shady areas. Overall, the effect of using texture in a garden is to create both visual and tactile interest.

Therefore it follows that if we have a bright pink fuchsia that we want to draw attention to, the contrasting dark foreground created by a purpleblack *Phormium* 'Platt's Black' planted in front it will highlight the fuchsia. So we can use contrasting colours not only to draw attention to specific plants but also to create excitement and visual stimulation in a planting scheme. Other successful contrasts in colour combinations are orange and purple, and blue and yellow.

Contrasting colours are, by their very nature, more stimulating and exciting to look at. Therefore a planting scheme of contrasting colours will leave a much stronger mental picture than a softer planting scheme. This is fine if this is the desired intention; however, the old adage 'less is more' is never better applied than when contrast is used with caution. A planting scheme full of strongly contrasting plant colours runs the risk of appearing messy and a jumble of strong colour, because the eye and the mind have to work so much

Balance

Balance is an aspect of planting that needs to be

A smooth, reflective hosta leaf.

achieved not only between planting and structure, but also between the plants themselves. The balance is struck between plant dimensions (height and width) and also between plant shapes. A general rule of thumb is to place taller plants at the rear of the border and decrease plant heights towards the front of the border. However, this 'rule' can be modified and taller 'see through' plants placed nearer the front of the border. Take, for example, a mature hedge. Part of the hedge dies, leaving a gap; this may be filled with a younger plant, but the hedge will always look out of balance in this area, due to the difference in size between the new planting and the old. The planting designer also seeks to achieve a balance of planting interest throughout the seasons. Balance is explored further in Chapter 2.

Unity

Unity is a broad term that, when it is achieved, describes a planting scheme that appears as a whole, a cohesive unit in which every single plant plays its part, none being particularly more dominant than the others. That is not to say that a variety of colours and/or plant shapes cannot be used; when chosen with care the overall effect can still be one of unity. It is interesting to note here that unity is a combination of all of the planting design principles brought together in balance. If one principle is removed, the result will be a planting scheme that seems to be missing something. Sometimes we can look at a border or bed and find ourselves saying 'Well, I like it but...' We cannot define exactly what it is that the scheme is lacking, but we instinctively know that it is just not quite right – it lacks unity. If we look to the design principles and apply them, it is highly likely that the missing component will be recognized.

THE ORGANIC ELEMENT

As we have discovered, planting design is something of an umbrella term, covering a whole range of considerations and aspects.

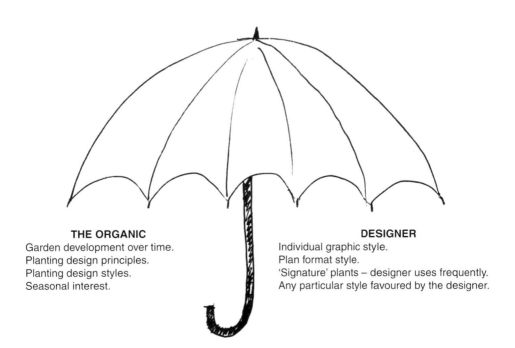

THE ORGANIC
Garden development over time.
Planting design principles.
Planting design styles.
Seasonal interest.

DESIGNER
Individual graphic style.
Plan format style.
'Signature' plants – designer uses frequently.
Any particular style favoured by the designer.

The planting design umbrella.

Having looked at the more theoretical aspects of the planting design principles and established a framework, are there any other concepts that we should consider when commencing work on a planting scheme? There are, and they can broadly be divided into two sections: 'the organic', which relates to the living, developing aspects of a garden; and 'the graphic', which relates to the individual designer style.

We look first at the organic element. This is an aspect of planning and designing the planting for a garden that in its very nature is ever evolving. In the spring we invariably look at our gardens and reassess and review them, not just because we are pleased or displeased with the previous season's 'performance', but also because the improved weather draws us to do something outside in the fresh air; this normally involves tidying the garden, to a greater or lesser extent, after the ravages of winter. This is a 'must do' requirement for the long-term health and success of the garden, whether it is done by a professional gardener/designer or simply by a person who likes to look after their own garden. Therefore it is important that, at whatever level we operate, there is a certain understanding of how plants and trees are going to perform as a whole, as a group of living, developing plants, each with its own unique characteristics and growth habit.

It is useful to divide these 'organic' planting design choices into two categories: individual plant characteristics, and horticultural requirements.

Plant characteristics

The characteristics of a plant include its form; its foliage (the texture, whether it is evergreen or deciduous, and its colour and season); whether it is a deciduous herbaceous flowering plant that dies down in the autumn; whether it is a flowering bulb, shrub or herbaceous plant; its colour and season; and what will be its eventual height and width. The successful planting scheme seeks to achieve a balance of :

- Flower colour: early and late spring, summer, autumn, winter

- Foliage colour: particularly relevant for autumnal interest
- Berries: late summer, autumn and winter interest
- Form: variety of plant shapes and sizes
- Evergreens providing interest throughout the seasons, but particularly winter form
- Architectural plant shapes that also provide strong winter form

The end result of considering these choices, and selecting a palette of plants that fulfil all these criteria, will be what I would consider a successful planting scheme that provides something of interest throughout the year, sprinkled with some points of particular interest. However, this is very subjective: what is attractive to one person will not be attractive to another. So how do we reconcile this dilemma? I would suggest that as long as the garden owner/client is happy and enjoys the planting in the garden, then the end goal has been achieved.

Horticultural requirements

Plant choice will be determined by soil type, which varies from one area to another. There are soil types that are specific to certain areas: the Cotswolds, for example, have a chalky/limey soil, while in other areas the soil may be more acidic. Both types of soil require plants that will tolerate their particular acidity or alkalinity, which is known as the soil pH. The soil pH scale ranges from 1–14; acid soils have a pH value below 7; alkaline soils have a pH value above 7; and neutral soils are pH7.

In addition to the determination of soil pH, the soil 'type' needs to be established. Broadly speaking, there are five soil types, as recognized and defined by the Royal Horticultural Society (RHS):

Sandy soil: light and free draining, often low fertility.
Peaty soil: acidic, low fertility, moist, often poorly drained.
Clay soil: fertile, often heavy, claggy and prone to waterlogging.

Calcareous soil: alkaline, free draining, often moderately fertile.

Silty soil: moderately fertile, but prone to compaction.

Other questions to ask about a plant's requirements include the following:

- Which aspect, sun or shade, does it prefer?
- Is the plant hardy or tender?
- Does the plant need a dry or a moisture-retentive soil?
- What are the drainage properties of the soil?
- Does the plant have particular pruning requirements? This is a 'must' consideration in the case of a client requiring a low maintenance garden, so that we do not introduce plants that require complicated pruning regimes.

A balance can be struck between fulfilling the horticultural requirements of a plant and the plant bringing its own character to the planting scheme as a whole; this is done by choosing the plant firstly for its compatibility with the given growing environment, and secondly for its specific characteristics such as shape, colour and so on. When this approach is taken to plant choice, something magical happens and the planting scheme 'works'; it is not just pleasing to look at but also thrives and therefore looks even better because it is healthy. The plant has been considered from two very different perspectives, which take into account everything it has to offer.

When plants are chosen on the basis of 'how they look' in isolation, with minimal consideration, if any, being given to how they are going to perform within the context of the existing garden, the result is a somewhat random effect to the planting, with no sense of unity and cohesion. It is for this reason that many people are dissatisfied with their garden, because plants are purchased individually at the garden centre, forgetting that what is found attractive is one plant, in isolation,

in a pot. Choosing a plant for its characteristics and then considering how it will perform with the other plants is a major contributory factor to the overall success of a planting scheme, together with giving due consideration to the plant's growing requirements. So what should we be thinking about when selecting or purchasing a plant?

Basic considerations

- What group does the plant belong to: tree, shrub, herbaceous perennial or bulb? This gives an indication of the eventual size of the plant and its individual growth habit and characteristics, essential if the planting scheme is to be 'fit for purpose' in the long term.
- The seasonal interest factor: does it flower, and if so, when?
- What colour are the flowers?
- Will it die down in the winter? Usually applied to the herbaceous perennial group,

Flowering on bare stems in late winter, early spring: *Chaenomeles speciosa* 'Nivalis'.

which goes through a complete life cycle in a year: it shoots, flowers, sets seed and dies down within a season and the cycle is repeated every year. This is an important consideration, as a space will be left where the plant has died down.

- Does it have attractive berries and/or foliage colour in the autumn?
- Is it evergreen, therefore giving permanent 'form' to the garden because it retains its leaves in the winter?
- Is it deciduous, meaning it will shed its leaves in the autumn? Very often deciduous shrubs will give stunning colour in the autumn in the form of foliage and then the bare stems will provide quite architectural structure through the winter. The *Cornus* group provides wonderful autumn and winter interest through their brightly coloured stems, which are particularly effective when planted as a group, or repeat planted around the garden. Some

The highly scented, late winter/early spring flowers of *Chimonanthus praecox* 'Grandiflorus'.

shrubs, such as *Chaenomeles* and *Chimonanthus praecox*, flower on their bare stems in late winter and very early spring, providing interest at a predominantly bare time of the year. The flowers are highly scented to attract the few insects around at this time of year.

- Most importantly, how big will it get? This cannot be stressed enough!

Sadly, on many occasions I have had to advise a client that one or more overgrown, poorly managed shrubs will have to be hard pruned in order to bring them back into order and render the garden manageable in the long term. Inevitably, this means that there will be a period of time when the garden or parts of it look decidedly unattractive, which is of course most undesirable and somewhat disagreeable to the client. However, this situation can be avoided by following some very simple ground rules when purchasing and planting new plants, particularly shrubs:

- Choose a shrub that will not get too big for its allotted space.
- Once the plant is established (which should be within a season), the application of a formative pruning regime will ensure a healthy framework to which an annual pruning regime can be applied, therefore avoiding the necessity to hard prune and leave a bare space.

These are simple, but none the less significant, considerations in the plant choice process and are but a few of the questions that we should be asking when choosing a plant, whether as an amateur or professional.

Plant density

Many plants, particularly in the herbaceous group, perform far better in terms of aesthetics when their selection is kept to a limited number of varieties, and those chosen varieties are planted as groups or drifts, providing maximum impact with regard to colour, shape and seasonal interest. This is one of the most significant aspects of planting design and if executed successfully will

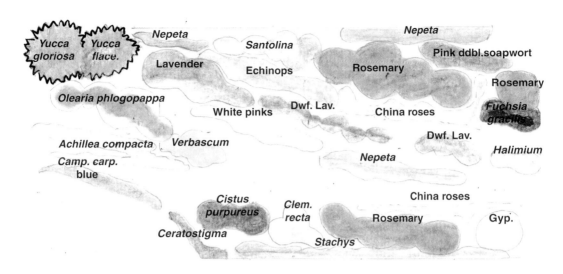

A Jekyll style planting plan, using watercoloured, labelled drifts. Note the loose, relaxed style. Her labelling, however, was handwritten.

result in a planting scheme that not only has an element of interest all year round but also appears as a whole, with a sense of unity. This is because the plant palette has been controlled and the selected plants can each display their individual characteristics. It is not unlike an orchestra, where each instrument plays its own set piece without dominating the others, and the result is a harmonious piece of music. To take the analogy further, if an instrument plays a wrong note, it is very quickly recognized and can be disruptive and off-putting to the rest of the orchestra. In the same way, if we were to place a scarlet plant in a planting scheme of soft pinks and blues, for example, it would immediately command attention and dominate, because its colour is so different and in strong contrast to what is around it.

General maintenance

An essential element of planting design, to which great attention should be paid, is general maintenance. Significantly, this is not just about keeping the garden weed-free; more importantly, it involves assessing the garden as a developing, organic commodity, and the subsequent changes over time that will undoubtedly take place. This does require the ability to *visualize* what the garden and individual plants will look like in the future. A notable example of this can be seen in the work of Capability Brown, who was famous for his many grand landscape schemes. In his planting of large areas of parkland he used groups of large trees, strategically placed to be viewed from a variety of positions within the house. This required the 'vision' to know what those trees would look like when fully grown, although they would not actually reach maturity in his lifetime.

To enable you to develop this skill and knowledge, when you list plants note down their growth and flowering habits. This is particularly successful when notes are included around the planting scheme, which has been 'sketched' using the plant shapes; we will consider this in more detail in Chapter 6, 'The Plant Shapes Method'.

Awareness and insight into how the garden is going to look when mature is therefore going to impact upon and strongly influence the choice of plant. For example, if you have a space one metre wide, it would be a pointless exercise to specify a *Viburnum tinus*, an evergreen, spring-flowering shrub that will reach up to ten feet and more at

A planting plan in traditional format.

'Hill End House'

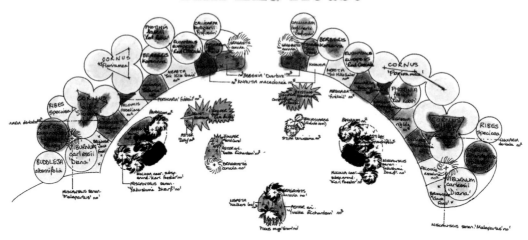

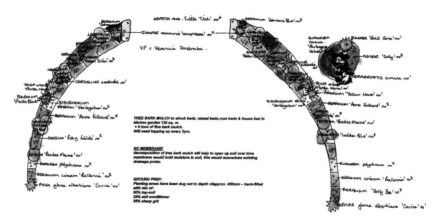

PLANT SCHEDULE - Project: 'HILL END HOUSE' Mr & Mrs Williams   (RB = Raised Bed, SB = Shrub Bed, GB = Gravel Bed)

Qu	Size	Variety	Unit Price	Total Price	Qu	Size	Variety	Unit Price	Total Price
	2L	**HERBACEOUS**			6	2L	Nepeta 'Little Titch' RB		
6		Astilbe arendsii 'Fanal' (shrub bed)			4		Phlomis russeliana SB		
5		Astilbe arendsii 'Snowdrift' SB			4		Persicaria amplex. 'Firetail' SB		
5		Aster ericoides 'Yvette Richardson' GB			8		Scabiosa 'Helen Dillon' SB		
6		Aster n.b. 'Dolly' GB			6		Sedum 'Ruby Glow' RB		
6		Bergenia overture GB			10		Sisyrinchium striatum variegatum RB		
6		Brunnera microphylla 'Jack Frost' SB			9		Verbena bonariensis SB		
4		Cirsium rivulare 'Atropurpureum' SB			2		Verbena 'Homestead Purple' SB		
5		Diascia 'Ruby Fields' RB			5		Verbena rigida SB		
4		Euphorbia carach. 'Portugese Velevet' GB			6		Veronica longifolia 'Royal Candles' RB		
5		Euphorbia polychrome GB			10		Veronica prostrate RB		
6		Geranium cinerium 'Ballerina' RB					**GRASSES.**		
6		Geranium 'Anne Folkard' RB			5		Eragrostis curvula GB		
12		Geranium 'Johnsons Blue' (kitchen gdn)			2		Miscanthus sen. 'Yakushima Dwarf' GB		
4		Geranium 'Jolly Bee' RB			2		Molinia caer.sub.arund. 'Karl Foester' GB		
6		Geranium phaeum 'Mrs. Kendal Clark' KG			2		Molinia caer.subsp.c. 'Moorhexe' GB		
10		Geranium 'Anne Folkard' KG			1		Miscanthus sen. 'Flamingo' GB		
10		Knautia macedonica			2		Miscanthus senen. 'Malepartus' SB		
4		Ligularia dentata 'Desdemona' SB			4		Pannicum virg. 'Squaw' GB		
14		Lychnis chalcedonica SB			3		Stipa gigantea SB		
4		Monarda 'Balance' SB			3		Stipa tenuissima GB		
12		Nepeta 'Six Hills Giant' SB					Hardy ferns x 6 (on nursery)		
3		Nepeta 'Walkers Low' GB							

ANY SUBSTITUTIONS PLEASE CALL CAROL SMITH ON Tel/Fax 01905 427120, Mob. 0774 7788543

PLANT SCHEDULE - Project: 'HILL END HOUSE' MR. & MRS. WILLIAMS.

Qu	Size	Variety	Unit Price	Total Price	Qu	Size	Variety	Unit Price	Total Price
		TREES.			2	3L	Viburnum carlessii 'Diana' SB		
2		Acer 'Crimson King' 1800 ht					**CONIFERS.**		
2		Amelanchier lamarkii 1800 ht			2	7.5L	Juniper conferta 'Blue Pacific' GB		
2		Liquidamber orientale 1800 ht			2	7.5L	Juniper communis 'Gold Cone' GB		
3		Betula 'Jacquemontii' multi-stem 1800ht			2	7.5L	Juniper communis 'Compressa' RB		
1		Acer palmatum 'Bloodgood' 600/800			1	7.5L	Pinus mugo 'Gnom' GB		
1		Acer palmatum 'Okushimo' 600/800			2	3L	Picea glauca albertiana 'Conica' RB		
		SHRUBS.			2	7.5L	Thuja orientalis 'Aurea Nana' RB		
1	3L	Buddlejah alternifolia SB					**PHORMIUMS**		
2		Berbebris koreanna SB			1	3L	Phormium 'Platts Black' RB		
6		Cornus alba sibirica SB			1	3L	Phormium 'Yellow Wave' RB		
6		Cornus 'Flaviramea' SB							
2		Cercis canandensis 'Forest Pansy' SB							
2		Callicarpa bodinerii 'Profusion' SB							
2		Cordyline australis SB							
2		Euonymus europeus 'Red Cascade' SB							
2		Erysium 'Bowles Mauve' 'RB							
1		Fatsia japonica KB							
100		Lavendula angust. 'Hidcote' (dwarf hedge)							
18		Lavendula angust. 'Loddon Blue' (raised beds)							
2		Photinia fraserii 'Red Robin' (on nursery)							
2		Pittosporum 'Tom Thumb' SB							
2		Ribes Speciosa SB							

CS... *garden*design

DATE: 16/10/06

PLAN: Planting Plan -
Shrub beds
Gravel garden
Raised beds

SCALE: 1 : 50

CLIENT:
Mr. & Mrs Williams
'Hilland House'
Station Road
Bransford
Worcs. WR6 5JJ

TEL: 01905 831863

A planting plan with colour.

maturity. Obviously, it is going to outgrow the allotted space within five years unless you plan to apply a regular pruning regime that will keep the shrub within the growing space. Alternatively, you could choose a slower-growing shrub whose ultimate size is smaller; either at the point of specification or when the space is overcrowded and remedial measures are necessary. There are consequences to our choices; if we make the correct and appropriate choices through planning and consideration, these will be minimal and therefore the garden will reach its peak of perfection and potential in the fullness of time, rather than becoming a series of garden maintenance problems.

DESIGNER/GRAPHIC STYLE

In complete contrast to this 'organic' aspect of planting design is the element of individual designer style. Each designer tends to develop not only their own unique graphic style for drawings and planting plans, but also a planting style that will favour the use of certain so-called signature plants and colours. These key elements will lead to a particular designer's work being almost instantly recognizable. The work of Piet Oudolf comes to mind, with its use mainly of grasses planted in large drifts, with certain herbaceous perennials for colour and additional interest.

To demonstrate a particular planting plan and planting style, we need look no further than at the work of Gertrude Jekyll, who used water-colour paints when designing a planting scheme. She planned planting schemes by producing paintings in which initially she chose particular colours to represent drifts of flowers, using a selection of either contrasting or harmonizing colours. Using watercolour paints in this way provided her with a highly 'visual' impression of what the intended scheme would look like when eventually planted. Once she had achieved the colour balance she desired, she chose plant varieties, and then transformed the paint colours into plants. Her schemes contained high numbers of herbaceous perennials which, when they had died down, were superseded by strong, structural elements such as evergreen hedging, to provide form during the winter months and a dark backdrop during the summer months. A typical Jekyll planting plan is a work of art in which plants are represented by hand drawn, irregular shapes of colour with the plant names noted around the edge.

This is a method that can be used by both the enthusiastic gardener and designer, in order to explore and define the preferred colour palette for the planting. The illustrations earlier in this chapter show other examples of planting plans and planting styles.

In this chapter we have looked at a wide variety of aspects of planting design, from the theoretical to the practical. All of them are equally important and it is worth taking time to understand their individual contribution to a successful planting scheme.

2 PLANT USE

The striking paeony, of which there are many varieites, can be used as a short-lived focal point plant.

'Plant use' explores *how* plants can be used in the garden, the process by which plants are chosen for specific qualities. For example, an evergreen climber is selected primarily for its ability to remain green throughout the winter months, and for its vertical growth habit. This quality is then combined with strategic *positioning* to have the resulting effect of creating a permanent screen. Thus the climber has not been selected for its more aesthetic qualities, such as flower colour, but for its ability to perform a certain *function*.

It is by exploring this aspect of plants that we begin to see them in a very different way and to choose them for much broader reasons than simply how pretty they look.

CONSIDERATIONS IN PLANT USE

Plant spacing and plant dimensions

Plant spacing, in this instance, is not about calculating how many plants are required for a

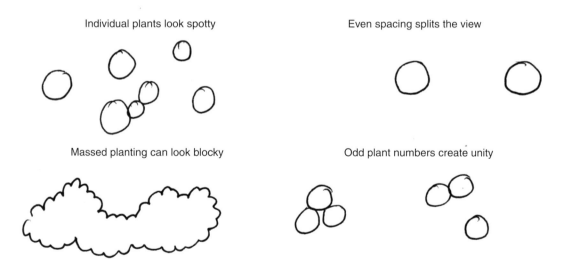

Manipulate people's movement around the garden

Draw the eye to:
A particular view
A point of interest
A focal point

PLANT USE CONSIDERATIONS – focus on 'how' plants perform in the garden/ landscape. Plants can be used to…

Control the way in which a person views the garden

Create perspective

Draw people through a sequence of spaces

Give tasters – tempt people to explore

Plant use considerations.

Individual plants look spotty

Even spacing splits the view

Massed planting can look blocky

Odd plant numbers create unity

certain area, but about the variety of effects that can occur by creating space between plants. We shall consider them as three-dimensional objects with width, depth and height which, when introduced into a space, ultimately change the nature of the space, and also look at how the planting space available to us can be used. As these effects are visual, this is best explained through illustrations.

Plant use and visual line

Positioning/placement

The strategic positioning of plants is just one

For further consideration – wasted space between plant groups

Space available under trees

Plant spacing.

The plants are all the same height

The effect is a lack of visual interest and the plants' individual charcteristics are not displayed.

Variety of heights provides more visual interest.

The effects of height.

Horizontals add breadth.

Scattered evergreens break
the composition and create rhythm.

Clustered evergreens unify a
scheme and provide a different
appearance in winter.

Permanent shape and form.

aspect of 'plant use'. Plants can be placed/positioned to create specific effects within a garden, stimulating our sense of 'spatial awareness'. They can be used in such a way that they give a different visual impression of the space to what is actually there. For example, a narrow garden can be made to feel and look wider by planting a hedge across its width; this makes the eye travel from one side of the garden to the other, giving the impression of width, rather than the eye looking down the length of the garden from the house to the rear boundary, which accentuates how narrow it is.

Traffic control

In addition to creating visual/spatial effects, plants can be used in such a way that they control the movement of people within a garden, almost like a traffic control system. It is a strange concept for us to understand that 'people movement' in gardens is controlled, and has been for as long as gardens have existed. When walking around a garden we have no sense of 'being controlled', but simply by following a designated pathway, the route by which we walk through the garden and experience it is being controlled. This example refers to hard landscaping such as paths, the main purpose of which is to provide us with functional surfaces that prevent shoes from carrying mud and dirt into the house. However, the same can be said of plant use, which has the same motive of controlling movement and experience.

Desire lines

The phrase 'desire lines' describes the human 'desire' to take the shortest route from A to B, whether or not this means wearing a path through the middle of a lawn! By creating a planted border around the lawn, the user is deterred and forced to take a route around it. Interestingly, the plants do not have to be tall; short, knee-high planting will have the same deterrent effect: plants are being used to control movement. A classic example of this is the traditional parterre bed, surrounded by dwarf hedging. This not only looks attractive by creating ground pattern and defining the parterre and its contents, but by creating a physical barrier, the

A traditional parterre bed.

dwarf hedge has the effect of preventing people from walking on the bed.

The more complicated the pattern, the more skilled the gardener – a reflection of the owners' financial prowess which was typical of the values of the formal culture of the Victorian era. Today we still see the same technique applied to summer bedding displays in public parks and on traffic roundabouts.

Particularly in public gardens, or private gardens open to the public, movement is still generally controlled today in order to guide people around on the route that the owner/designer wishes. This may be to direct them towards a particularly beautiful vista or focal point, or to take a specific route around the garden in order to experience it in a certain way. Of course there is also the practical aspect of keeping people off planted areas to ensure their continued growth and beauty.

The well-known garden at Hidcote employs 'plant use' to the full, with its series of enclosed 'rooms' created by tall evergreen hedges. The hedges prevent the visitor from seeing the entire garden, so that glimpses through a clipped archway to the next room draw people through and around the garden. The arches allow a peek through into the 'room' beyond, which stimulates a sense of curiosity, and therefore the movement of the viewer is, very subtly, being controlled.

Clipped hedging creating division and rooms at Hidcote.

So we can see that plants are not just an aesthetic commodity, but can also be used to change the experience of the space and to control how the space is used.

HEDGING AND SCREENING

Hedging is the use of plants to provide a living, possibly evergreen screen; it can be evergreen or

A clipped hedge archway.

A clipped evergreen hedge.

An unclipped
deciduous
hedge.

deciduous, flowering, dwarf or tall, clipped or unclipped.

The use of the hedge as a boundary marker goes back at least as far as 1000BC, when people began to want to define the boundaries and protect the land that they either owned or worked. It was a declaration of ownership or, if the territory was not owned, a mark that this was the piece of land upon which a group lived and from which they grew their food.

Before farming, when people were hunter-gatherers, hedges were made from dead, usually spiky, sharpened branches and twiggy growth to prevent attack. Hedging also acted as a barrier to livestock, separating animals from edible crops that the farmer grew for his own use. A further, more recent, use of hedging is to create a windbreak with the evergreen leylandii in order to protect crops from wind scorch. Thus many of the hedges that we see today have been in existence for hundreds, if not thousands, of years and human beings have adapted the use of hedging for modern purposes.

Screening and other functions

Plants that climb and flower, such as the *Clematis* family, can be grown up trellis to provide a flow-

---

THE USES OF PLANTS

Plants can be used to:

- Screen tall buildings and objects.
- Change the shape of a building.
- Link buildings and features together.
- Soften the walls of a building.
- Soften fencing.

---

ering, semi-transparent screen and creating division and vertical planting interest in a garden. Evergreens such as *Hedera* (ivy) and *Trachelospermum* (evergreen jasmine) are further options, grown up fencing and walls to soften the structure.

Spatial awareness: the experience of space

Spatial awareness is, very simply, an experience and awareness of the objects in the space around us, whether in a room or a garden. As a result of the sensory perception of our surroundings, it is also an awareness of our body's position in space,

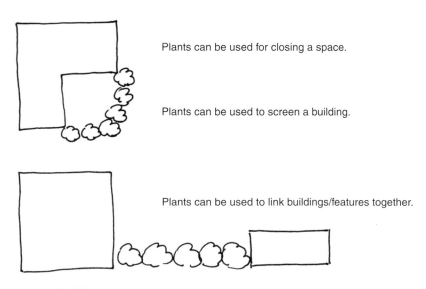

Plants can be used for closing a space.

Plants can be used to screen a building.

Plants can be used to link buildings/features together.

Plants and buildings.

IMPLIED/SUGGESTED SPACE

Mown grass

The edge of the mown grass implies a boundary.

Concept of spatial awareness and boundaries.

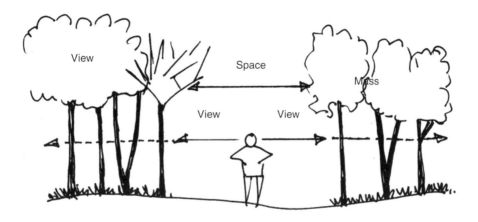

View

Space

Mass

View   View

The mass/bulk of the trees = implied space; the space is defined by the trunks but with views out.

Space and the effects of mass.

something that we become particularly aware of when in an outdoor space.

When standing in a garden considering its potential for planting options, one of the first things we notice will be the character of the space, which will become known to us as a series of 'feelings' about the garden. The Latin phrase '*genius loci*' describes this beautifully as 'the spirit of the place'. Does the garden feel large, open and expansive, or dark, bleak and cold, or inviting and relaxing, and so on? The qualities that we detect are the result of physical shape and size, colour, textures – the characteristics of the plants and hard landscaping within the garden; and all of these sensory qualities contribute to and affect our experience of the garden. Space is not unlike colour: as with red equating with heat, we begin to sense the essence of a space almost instantly, before we start to notice the finer details that make it up.

A group of plants creates a 'spatial composition' and will affect the experience of the garden

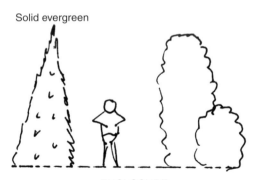

ENCLOSURE
Dense, evergreen plants above head height –
vision is taken forward.

SEMI-ENCLOSED
Decidious, light canopied planting – vision is
taken to right.

Mass – evergreen and deciduous.

Knee-high vegetation = implied boundary and limits movement, but it feels like an open space.

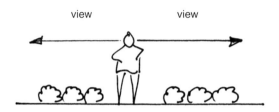

Blocked view on right, enclosure on right. Against planting – good position for a seat.

Mass and views.

space. For example, if the garden is surrounded by a 10ft-tall dark, evergreen hedge, it is more than probable that the garden will feel dark, confined and gloomy, and a sense of entrapment may be experienced. The composition of the hedge (its height, width and colour) is directly affecting the nature of the space and how it is perceived.

A garden is a natural space which the owner will have developed to a greater or lesser extent by making a series of decisions; these decisions will have been influenced primarily by the owner's functional requirements of the garden, closely followed by his or her aesthetic requirements.

Visual line
Even the direction in which a person looks in a garden can be controlled; the diagrams above demonstrate a variety of ways in which this is done.

Plants can be used as a permanent backdrop.

Plants can be used to create perspective.

Plants and objects.

Plants and objects

Some of the ways in which we use plants for a specific effect are everyday occurrences, but we do not recognize them as 'the way in which a plant is being used', we tend instead to recognize the complete picture. For example, we see a statue in front of an evergreen hedge; what is actually there, from a plant use perspective, is an evergreen hedge that is being used as a permanent backdrop to the statue.

In the diagram above, trees are being used to create perspective and a visual line to the statue. In the absence of the trees, the statue would appear to float in the space and its significance as part of the scene would be lost.

This is the very essence of plant use: it is about the end effect created, not just in terms of a cleverly considered function of the chosen planting, but how that planting has been executed.

Planting as a backdrop.

The use of colour combinations results in a successful planting scheme with a high level of visual appeal.

3 PLANTING DESIGN

In order to develop the ability to recognize what is not satisfactory in a garden, we need to assess not only how the plants within a given scheme are functioning, but also the aesthetic qualities of the scheme. The questions discussed in this chapter are specifically focused on this aspect of a planting scheme and form a useful framework within which to analyse either an existing or proposed planting scheme. Our focus will be, first, on plant aesthetics, and then on some of the practicalities of producing a planting plan.

Planting design is a broad term that covers a wide variety of aspects of a planting scheme, from the planting style to the given garden environ-

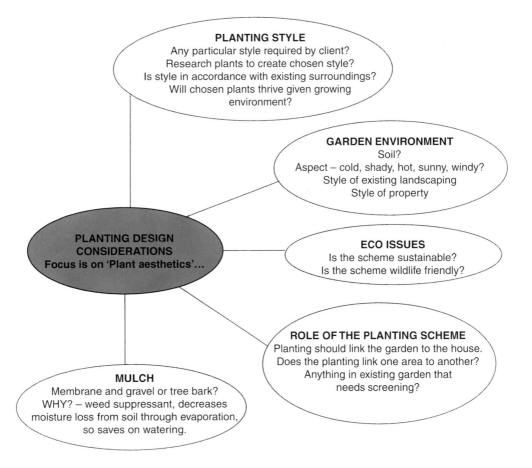

PLANTING STYLE
Any particular style required by client?
Research plants to create chosen style?
Is style in accordance with existing surroundings?
Will chosen plants thrive given growing
environment?

GARDEN ENVIRONMENT
Soil?
Aspect – cold, shady, hot, sunny, windy?
Style of existing landscaping
Style of property

PLANTING DESIGN CONSIDERATIONS
Focus is on 'Plant aesthetics'...

ECO ISSUES
Is the scheme sustainable?
Is the scheme wildlife friendly?

ROLE OF THE PLANTING SCHEME
Planting should link the garden to the house.
Does the planting link one area to another?
Anything in existing garden that
needs screening?

MULCH
Membrane and gravel or tree bark?
WHY? – weed suppressant, decreases
moisture loss from soil through evaporation,
so saves on watering.

Planting design considerations.

ment and ecological issues. Like individual ingredients in a recipe, these aspects need to be carefully thought through in the process of designing a planting scheme, in order to come up with the best scheme possible for the site. You will notice that these considerations are not just about the plants themselves, but extend further to include elements of the existing garden property, and basic but none the less essential ecological considerations. You may wonder what mulch has got to do with planting design: I would suggest that it should be included as a planting design consider-

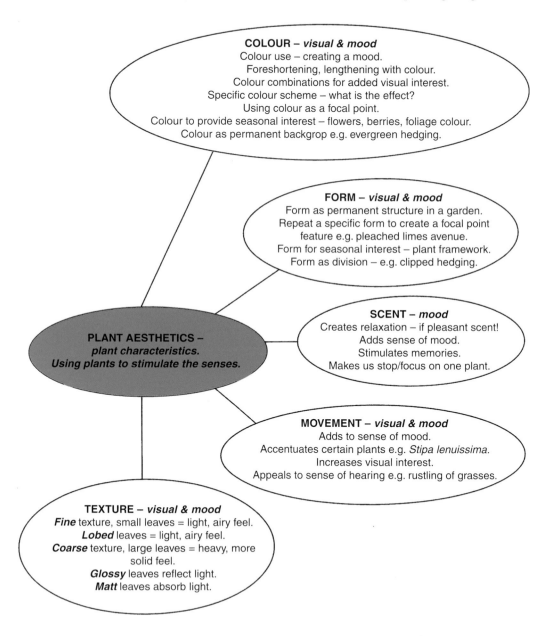

COLOUR – *visual & mood*
Colour use – creating a mood.
Foreshortening, lengthening with colour.
Colour combinations for added visual interest.
Specific colour scheme – what is the effect?
Using colour as a focal point.
Colour to provide seasonal interest – flowers, berries, foliage colour.
Colour as permanent backgrop e.g. evergreen hedging.

FORM – *visual & mood*
Form as permanent structure in a garden.
Repeat a specific form to create a focal point
feature e.g. pleached limes avenue.
Form for seasonal interest – plant framework.
Form as division – e.g. clipped hedging.

SCENT – *mood*
Creates relaxation – if pleasant scent!
Adds sense of mood.
Stimulates memories.
Makes us stop/focus on one plant.

PLANT AESTHETICS –
plant characteristics.
Using plants to stimulate the senses.

MOVEMENT – *visual & mood*
Adds to sense of mood.
Accentuates certain plants e.g. *Stipa lenuissima*.
Increases visual interest.
Appeals to sense of hearing e.g. rustling of grasses.

TEXTURE – *visual & mood*
Fine texture, small leaves = light, airy feel.
Lobed leaves = light, airy feel.
Coarse texture, large leaves = heavy, more
solid feel.
Glossy leaves reflect light.
Matt leaves absorb light.

Plant aesthetics.

ation because the application of a mulch will directly impact upon the health of the planting scheme by reducing evaporation from the soil surface and providing a 'blanket' for winter protection. It is therefore preferable to consider it at this stage rather than when the scheme is struggling and plant health has been damaged. Prevention is better than cure.

PLANT AESTHETICS

To clarify this aspect of planting design further, we need to define the word 'aesthetic'. The dictionary definition reads 'concerned with the beautiful', so, when used in relation to plants, we are placing our focus upon the 'beautiful' aspects of a plant or plants, which logically work hand in hand with their 'effects'. Therefore, by considering both of these, the designer 'uses' the plant to its maximum potential as well as providing the plant with the optimum growing conditions. Plant aesthetics can be divided into five main categories, as can be seen in the bubble chart above.

Plant height

Primarily, the plant shapes method draws heavily on the 'aesthetic qualities and effects' of the chosen plants. These aesthetic qualities include, amongst other aspects, the eventual size (that is, the approximate height and width) of the plant at maturity – maturity being estimated in the region of seven to ten years. This, of course, ensures that as far as is possible the proposed planting scheme will not have outgrown its allotted space in ten years' time. However, a word of caution: with today's changing weather patterns, and the resulting impact on plant growth rates, the stated 'eventual size' given by many books can only be regarded as a general guideline.

It is relevant at this point to explore plant height as a plant aesthetic in greater depth because it is the one aspect of planting design that the designer needs to get right from the offset. For example, if a border is 4ft wide, choosing to position a row of large shrubs to the rear of the border, with lower-growing herbaceous perenni-

als in front, is only going to result in short-lived success for the planting scheme. This is because the shrubs will eventually, within approximately three to five years, become large specimens and smother the shorter, lower-growing perennials – a mistake made by many people when purchasing plants.

At the design stage the problem can be avoided by using plants that are not going to grow too big, or by reducing the number of them and positioning a shrub at intervals, leaving clear spaces in between for the perennials to thrive. Often, when designers receive calls from the public complaining that their border is just 'not right', or 'it looks a mess', the problem frequently lies with shrubs that have far outgrown their allotted space. Correcting this does not neces- sarily mean removing the shrub; many shrubs can be hard pruned and will then, the following season, produce new shoots from the base. This new growth can then be kept in check and in accordance with the allocated space. For the purposes of designing a planting scheme, plant height can be further categorized as follows.

- **Tall:** above shoulder-height trees and shrubs, conifers and herbaceous perennials including grasses, usually used towards the back of the border. (NB some tall, see-through plants, such as *Stipa gigantea*, can be used mid-border or nearer to the front.)
- **Medium-tall:** above the waist but below the shoulder, Shrubs and tall herbaceous perennials including grasses.
- **Medium:** below the waist but above the knee; some shrubs, herbaceous perennials including grasses, and bulbs.
- **Small/short:** below knee-height plants, usually at the front of the border; some prostrate conifers, herbaceous perennials including grasses, heathers, and bulbs.
- **Ground cover:** ankle-height, at the front of the border and as permanent edging; some prostrate conifers, herbaceous perennials including grasses, and bulbs.

Plant height is an area of planting design that can

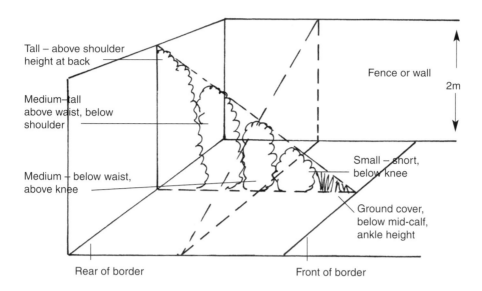

Tall – above shoulder height at back

Medium–tall above waist, below shoulder

Medium – below waist, above knee

Fence or wall

2m

Small – short, below knee

Ground cover, below mid-calf, ankle height

Rear of border

Front of border

The planting height triangle.

conform to traditional guidelines, as in the diagram above, but does not always have to.

This is a useful shape to memorize so that when assessing or designing a border the 'triangle' can be applied visually in the mind's eye, assisting the designer to recognize 'planting problems' with regard not only to plant heights but also plant width and depth. Categorizing the chosen plants into their respective size group provides a firm foundation upon which to make further plant choices.

The plant shapes method assists with this process, because the designer sketches the plant heights as seen in the mind's eye, using the fencing height (usually 2m) as a 'height indicator', thereby providing a visual outline of the proposed scheme.

Traditionally, the tallest plants were always placed at the back of the border and plant heights reduced towards the front of the border. However, when designing a planting scheme it can be creative to explore 'breaking' this rule and introducing taller plants towards the front of the border. In order for this to work, either the plant should have a loosely structured, see-through nature, or should be tall and narrow, so that

whatever is behind it can be seen. Some very interesting effects can be created by playing with plant heights in this way.

The designer can command attention to a specific plant and its surrounding area by using the aesthetic qualities of height and colour in conjunction with specific placement. The inclusion of some taller but 'see-through' planting, such as *Verbena bonariensis*, will create visual interest and height when used at the front of a border. The photograph opposite shows that an unexpected but none the less effective use of a tall plant, providing a see-through screen of vibrant lilac, can give a sense of depth to the border.

Less transparent plants with strong form, such as the tall and narrow *Cupressus sempervirens* (otherwise known as the Italian pencil cypress) or the shorter, more triangular-shaped *Thuja orientalis* 'Aurea Nana', can be used in the same way to draw attention onto that part of the border.

On occasions, simply moving plants around may be the required 'cure' to improve the aesthetic qualities of a border and increase its visual interest. However, it may require more drastic action, such as removing some of the plants that have become far too large or old and

ABOVE: See-through *Verbena bonariensis* with *Dahlia* 'Bishop of Llandaff'.

tired-looking and replacing them with something more suitable and increasing visual interest by introducing a strong shape or colour.

Other plant aesthetics

Colour

The formula 'colour = mood' should be given due respect when designing a planting scheme. We shall look at colour use in more detail in Chapter 7, but suffice to say at this point that colour is the strongest tool in the toolbox when working with plants. When considering plant aesthetics, the emphasis is on the *effect* of any chosen colours. If any mistake will be noticed almost immediately and commented upon, it is that of poor or eye-shocking use of colour. However, as I have previously mentioned, this is very subjective.

The eye is very sensitive to colour, both colour it is comfortable with and colour that is uncomfortable. I use the word 'comfort' intentionally, as there is a sense of discomfort when viewing colour that the eye and mind are not happy with. But there is nothing like the feeling of satisfaction brought about by looking at a beautiful colour

scheme. Colour also holds unspoken messages such as red = hot, blue = cool, so when including these colours in a scheme, the 'message' needs to be balanced if this is not the effect that we wish to impart. This is achieved by introducing other

Thuja orientalis 'Aurea Nana'.

Height used to define the rectangular line of the pool.

colours to moderate and balance the stronger colours in the scheme.

Form

Form is an 'aesthetic' that can be used to create high impact visual effect. Visualize a clipped copper beech hedge and compare the strength of this formal image with the softer image of an informal, unclipped, mixed hedge.

Form can be used to emphasize and strengthen a ground shape such as a circular lawn. *Cupressus sempervirens* planted around a circular lawn enhances and draws attention to the shape by its form and height.

Form is the designer's key tool for providing not only structural interest, but interest throughout the seasons. Plants that provide form within a planting scheme can be likened to the garden's unseen 'skeleton' or, as designers say, its 'framework', which when all else has disappeared for its winter rest, comes to the fore and provides us with interest through this otherwise potentially very 'flat' season in the garden.

The favoured plants for providing form are evergreens, architectural shapes, grasses and some deciduous plants. Of particular interest for its eye-catching, horizontal, tiered growth habit is *Viburnum plicatum* 'Mariesii'; not only does it provide the horizontal growth habit for structural winter interest, best seen with bare stems, it also follows this with layer upon layer of white hydrangea-like spring flowers and finishes with a flourish of orange/yellow autumn foliage. What a plant!

Scent

This again is an unseen but nonetheless incredibly powerful garden experience. Increasingly, research in the science of psycho-neuro-immunology shows that if we feel good and positive, our sense of well-being is enhanced and this in turn strengthens our immune system so that resistance to infection is considerably improved. Conversely, if we are low and depressed we produce a chemical messenger called cytokinin, which suppresses the immune system, increasing our vulnerability to infection. If we have high stress levels another type of cytokinin is produced, which over-stimulates the immune system, possibly to the point of breakdown. So there is a direct link between things that give us a sense of well-being and our health. Scent is recognized as being one of the most powerful of these stimulants, and it also has the power to trigger memory, usually positive memories associated with food! Scent from flowers and our individual response to it is somewhat more of a mystery, but none the less evocative.

In the cold grey months of January and February, how wonderful it is to breathe in the sweet, heady scent of an early flowering shrub such as *Sarcococca confusa*, hence its nickname 'Sweetbox'. Its scent more than makes up for its otherwise somewhat low visual impact.

It is almost an automatic response, when we detect a lovely scent in the air, to take a deep breath and release it with a deep sigh; this triggers deep relaxation of mind and body. Late winter and early spring flower scent gives us a sense of hope for the summer and sun to come, so our spirit is uplifted as well. The winter garden relies on form and scent for the greatest part of its interest.

Movement

Movement is a fascinating phenomenon that is not often considered as a separate requirement with regard to how it can be brought into a garden. It is something that we recognize visually; a comment regularly heard from garden visitors is, 'Isn't that wonderful, the way it sways in the breeze', but it is not something that people put on their list of plant attributes to be acquired when purchasing plants.

Movement can instil a deep sense of relaxation. Watching a swathe of light, airy grasses gently

Viburnum plicatum 'Mariesii'.

Sarcococca confusa with its tiny white, highly scented flowers.

sway in the breeze can be almost hypnotic as they gently rock from side to side. Visualize a meadow with a breeze, gently moving the grasses: it holds our attention visually as the patterns seen in the moving grass change in tandem with the breeze's direction. Movement is a crucial garden element and instils the garden with energy, reminding us of the unseen natural force of the wind.

The garden without movement appears very still and lacking in 'life'. Of course, with movement comes sound: the rustling of grasses and bamboos, the gentle trickle of a water feature rather than an intrusive gushing waterfall. Pleasant sounds bring us straight into the present moment to listen and watch. During these moments we detach from the ever-present 'head chatter' and become peaceful, which is why movement and sound are key in creating tranquillity in a garden.

Interestingly, in garden design movement is also about how *we* move *around* the garden. A gently, curving, meandering path gives rise to contemplation and relaxation, in strong contrast to a straight, angular pathway which gives rise to tension as we concentrate on where the path is turning next and negotiate the sharp turns. The same effect is experienced when looking at either a curved or a linear design plan, and often how a design works on paper is how it will work on the ground.

Grasses and bamboos are the favoured groups to provide movement; particularly fine examples are *Stipa tenuissima*, the *Miscanthus* family, and the *Panicums*.

SOME OF THE BEST EARLY SCENTED SHRUBS

- *Sarcococca humilis*
- *Chimonanthus praecox*
- *Choisya ternata*
- *Daphne*
- *Mahonia* x *media* 'Charity'
- *Hamamelis mollis*

GRASSES AND BAMBOOS FOR MOVEMENT

- *Stipa tenuissima*
- *Stipa arundinacea*, now known as *Anemanthele lessoniana* (Pheasant's tail grass)
- *Miscanthus sinensis* 'Gracillimus'
- *Miscanthus sacchariflorus*
- *Panicum virgatum*
- *Eragrostis curvula* (African love grass)
- *Pennisetum*
- *Phyllostachys nigra* (Black bamboo)
- *Phyllostachys aurea* (Golden bamboo)
- *Fargesia nitida*

Sound

Sound is another of those strange garden elements that would not be put on a wish list, but we do notice its absence. Most garden sounds arise from naturally occurring phenomena such as birdsong, frogs croaking, the hum of bees and so on. To raise our awareness and make us totally present in the garden, other sounds can be introduced which attract our attention, such as wind chimes, a water feature, rustling grasses and bamboos.

I would add a note of caution here: a water feature that gushes rather than trickles or wind chimes that clang rather than gently chime will only cause irritation as opposed to the intended 'relaxation' effect, so take care when choosing either of these.

Heavy traffic noise does not mean that a loud water feature is required; it is a surprising fact that a gently trickling water feature will damp down traffic noise because it diverts attention from the traffic to itself; masking undesirable noise is about distraction rather than volume.

Texture

If we liken texture in the garden to fabric, we get a strong visual impression of this 'aesthetic'. A fabric made from very thin, fine threads will appear as a fine texture and vice versa. In plants it is the surface quality of their leaves and flowers that dictates the perceived texture. Texture can be experienced through touch as well as sight, and can be thought of as surface texture and visual texture.

Surface texture involves the sense of touch; think of the large grey, felt-like leaves of *Verbascum olympicum* that make you want to stroke them, so that enjoyment is found in experiencing the differing leaf textures, from soft and asking to be stroked to smooth and glossy. The

Stipa tenuissima.

Ecological choices and their benefits

Choice	Benefit
Include nectar and pollen-rich plants.	Food source for bees, butterflies and other plant visiting insects.
Include fruiting trees and shrubs.	Food source for mammals and birds.
Include night-flowering and scented species.	Attracts moths and is a food source.
Use plant species that seed and produce young plants freely.	Reduction in plant production costs and carbon footprint.
Use plants that bulk up easily, 'splits' can then be used to increase plant numbers.	Reduction in plant production costs and carbon footprint.
Delay cutting back perennials until early spring.	Dead foliage will provide food and shelter for many insects.
Reduce the use of chemicals	Eco-friendly environment for insects and small mammals.
Consider leaving a part of the lawn uncut.	Long grass is beneficial to many species, and reduces fuel use and therefore emissions.
Consider introducing an area for wild flower meadow.	Food source for small mammals and insects.
Consider the use of a membrane and mulch.	Reduces water requirements; using a mulch, particularly tree bark, provides a food source and shelter for many insects.

surface texture of a leaf is affected by the way that light is reflected off it. A glossy, shiny leaf reflects more light so can appear smaller.

Visual texture is created by foliage size and density. Plants with widely spaced, large leaves will appear more 'coarse' than densely packed small leaves, which appear finer. Using a mixture of contrasting textures adds further interest to a planting scheme.

Eco-friendly planting

The phrase 'eco-friendly' sounds a little intimidating. It is a vast subject with some contentions, but for the purposes of planting design it can be simplified to some basic requirements which, if included as part of a planting scheme, will be eco-friendly.

Taking the extra time involved to research and choose plants that provide these benefits is well worth the effort when through the winter and spring increased numbers of birds visit the garden for food and nesting materials. During the summer the garden will positively buzz with increased insect and butterfly activity, and you will have the added satisfaction that you are 'doing your bit' to assist and support nature.

PRODUCING A PLANTING PLAN

The planting plan is a twofold document. It plays a role in demonstrating the proposed planting scheme to the client, especially when colour rendered, and also acts as a basic working document for the planting designer/contractor. The client can use the planting plan in conjunction with a plant maintenance schedule in order to carry out their own maintenance work.

A planting plan is drawn to scale, the most commonly used scales being 1:50 for a small to average sized garden, and 1:100 for larger areas. It has two functions: firstly, it is a way of 'organizing' the selected plants as the designer wishes them to be set out and planted, taking into account growth rates and eventual size at maturity; and secondly, it is a means of calculating plant quantities.

Whether amateur or professional, the planting plan is the process by which the planting of a selected area, or site, is *designed*: plant size, shape and colour, season of interest and positioning, are all given due consideration as the designer 'arranges' the plants on the plan. The plants will have been chosen prior to this stage and a plant schedule or plant list drawn up.

The plant schedule

This is the plant list in its final draft, and it can be handwritten or typed into a table that can then very easily be emailed to nursery suppliers for sourcing and costing. The plant schedule contains the list of plant names, along with details of the required pot size and quantity, information crucial to the ordering, selection and costing of the planting aspect of a project.

Planting plan graphics

The plants are represented using a variety of circles, drawn to scale to represent the plant size at maturity. So for a large shrub that is going to make a width of 1.8–2m in approximately seven to ten years, a circle is drawn of either 1.8m or 2m at 1:50. Circle sizes are altered according to the plants' eventual size. Plastic circle templates

are readily available at most art and office supply outlets.

Although in traditional planting plan graphics, all plants were represented by the circle method, plants that are used in larger quantities, usually herbaceous perennials and grasses, can be drawn in drifts and each plant marked with a cross, usually at 300–400mm spacing; the crosses can then be counted and plant quantities calculated. Using the drift style makes for a planting plan that is high impact when coloured, which in turn makes it easier for the client to imagine the colour scheme.

Labelling

Again traditionally, labelling was always around the outside of the planting plan, with ruled lines linking the label to the plant area. This always looks very smart but can be very difficult to follow when reading the plan on site. An alternative method is to use a combination of this method and plant names that are written directly onto the shrub or plant area, making the plan very easy to follow when setting out the plants on site.

The main criteria of a successful planting plan as a working document are twofold: it must be clear and easy to read, and it must have accurate information regarding plant names, pot sizes and plant numbers.

Contemporary planting using a combination of contrasting form, foliage shape and colour – large foliage tree ferns and hostas against the red and orange acer trees. Note the patio joints filled with fine foliage of 'mind-your-own-business'.

The combination of grasses with herbaceous perennials provides a distinctive naturalistic planting style.

4 PLANTING DESIGN STYLES

PLANTING STYLE

What is style when applied to planting design? The strongest images that immediately spring to mind and best demonstrate style are from the world of fashion. Hippie style, with its characteristic long hair, tie-dyed flowing clothing, headbands and lots of beads, is unique and in complete contrast to the Mods style of a smart fitted suit for male or female, worn with a button-down collared shirt and tie and short cut hair. Each of these styles is distinguished by its striking contrast of characteristics, and carries a strong visual image. It is no different in the world of planting style. Each garden style is defined by a collection of differing elements, both hard and soft landscaping, which when brought together are symbolic of a particular style; however, this book focuses on planting design, so the focus is on the plants of a particular style.

Where do these styles come from?

Gardens have evolved throughout history as a direct result of the social and cultural nuances of the day. Take, for example, vegetable growing. There were dramatic changes to landownership in the eighteenth and nineteenth centuries. Land-

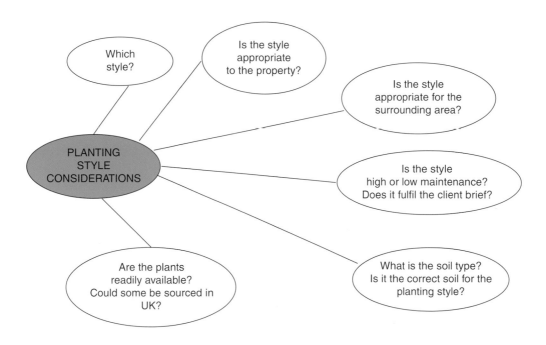

Planting style considerations.

owners were encouraged by the Enclosures Act of 1845 to define the boundaries and 'enclose' their land. This was followed by great unrest amongst the peasants, who were literally thrown off the land they had lived on and cultivated to eke out an existence. The rebellions gave rise to the Allotments Act of 1845, followed some time later by another historic event, the 'Dig for Victory' campaign of World War Two. Both of these societal and cultural events directly impacted upon land and garden use, culminating in the birth of allotments and Victorian kitchen gardens, in which the growing of vegetables for domestic rather than commercial use became the norm. Both allotments and Victorian kitchen gardens have a very strong sense of style, which when spoken or thought about produce an immediate mental image.

Other garden styles seen in Britain have been influenced by various European architectural and garden styles; the most influential of these are the Romanesque, the French and Italian Renaissance, and the Mediterranean.

Style and aspect

A garden style is achieved by the combination of both hard landscaping materials and plants. However, the sense of the chosen style will not be achieved by simply combining these two elements. There are other more subtle but none the less essential 'ingredients', one of the most important of these being 'aspect' – which way the garden or border faces. A general rule of thumb is that the more southerly a border faces, the more sun it will

> **A SELECTION OF PLANTING STYLES**
>
> - Mediterranean
> - Formal/informal
> - Traditional
> - Cottage
> - Contemporary
> - Architectural
> - Chinese/Japanese
> - Scree or gravel
> - Prairie
> - Colour schemed

receive; so a south-facing border will appear light, bright and 'sunny'. With certain planting styles, the correct marriage of 'aspect' and 'style' is imperative to the success of the border. For instance, a north-facing border planted in Mediterranean style would not succeed for two reasons. Firstly, from the perspective of horticultural needs, Mediterranean-type plants require full sun, so would certainly not thrive or even, possibly, survive in the cold shade of a north-facing border. Secondly, from a visual and psychological perspective, our minds would recognize the plants and connect them with being sun loving, and would then reject and question their position in shade; they just would not look right.

Feasibility

This is a major consideration when planning any planting, but particularly when embarking upon

Mediterranean-style planting.

Victorian-style planting, colour-schemed and mixed, with a clipped hedge backdrop.

a specific style. Whether the scheme is feasible or not will be influenced by three things:

- Soil type
- Availability of the requisite plants
- Hardiness

In the case of Mediterranean style, plants will require a free draining, almost sandy type of soil and, as already discussed, plenty of sun. Mediterranean-type plants are readily available, but this is dependent upon long-distance transportation; many of them are brought in on huge lorries from the Continent, so there are risks with the change of environment. With regard to the issue of hardiness, there are many beautiful and dramatic plants available to us, but you need to be as sure as possible that they will be tough enough to survive our long, cold, and (when not cold) wet winters. If they will not survive outdoors, then provision has to be made for them to be under cover, possibly in a costly heated structure over winter.

The designer's skills may be tested when an unrealistic brief is received from the client for a style of planting that is inappropriate for the given growing environment. In this situation designers should be able to draw upon their knowledge base and people skills and advise a planting style that is appropriate for the given garden aspect and environment.

Mediterranean

Characteristics
- Sunshine and good light.
- Strong colours.
- Architectural plants.
- Use of pots, patterned mosaic.
- Possibly white walls.

Mediterranean style plants
Cordyline australis
Agapanthus
Geraniums
Succulents
Herbs such as thyme, rosemary and marjoram
Bouganvillea 'Purple King' (if in a south-facing, sheltered spot, will need over winter protection)
Bay (*Laurus nobilis*)
Trachycarpus
Olive (*Olea europaea*)
Campsis (a climber with vibrant trumpet-shaped flowers)
Cupressus sempervirens (can brown if exposed to too much wind).

Formal

Both the formal and informal styles are predominantly governed by the hard landscaping layout, rather than the use of specific plants.

Characteristics
- Strong form, usually evergreen.
- Clipped topiary.
- Clipped hedging.
- Often clipped dwarf hedging to edge the borders.
- Often linear, square-shaped beds and borders.
- Traditional planting mix: shrubs at back and perennial herbaceous plants.
- Traditional bedding plant schemes in summer (echoes of Victorian style).

Informal

Characteristics
- Very relaxed planting of loose drifts of mixed colour; soft, pastel colours are easier on the eye.
- Use of grasses to add movement.
- Beds and borders often in sinuous curves.

Traditional

Characteristics
- A mix of traditional plants from the main groups of shrubs, herbaceous perennials and bulbs, with others such as roses, climbers and conifers.
- Planted in a traditional way with height at the back of the border reducing towards the front of the border.
- Roses and climbers, if planted on an obelisk or scrambling over an archway, give a strong impression of a traditional garden.
- Heathers may be included, but only of course if the soil is acidic.
- Plants such as phormiums, cordylines and grasses, which are more strongly associated with twentieth-century style, would not be used. (Of course this is debatable, as cordylines have been in use since Victorian times; however, they do bring a strong sense of Mediterranean and architectural planting to any scheme.)

Cottage

Characteristics
- Loose, informal planting.
- Mixed colours, randomly distributed througout.
- High maintenance due to the high numbers of herbaceous perennials used.
- Spring and summer are main seasons of interest.
- Planted containers dotted around.

Cottage style plants
Mixed field hedging
Spring bulbs
Old English lavender
Herbaceous perennials
Leucanthemum
Hollyhocks
Sunflowers

Tall lupins in a
cottage-style border.

Delphiniums
Climbers – should scramble up the wall, porch, over arches
Honeysuckle (*Lonicera*)
Jasminum officinale
Clematis
Roses such as Paul's Himalayan Musk (1848) – vigorous and graceful with dainty, scented flowers; or the Noisette rose 'Gloire de Dijon' (1853)
Herbs: *Rosmarinus officinalis* (rosemary), *Salvia officinalis* (sage), thymes
White phlox
Dianthus – old-fashioned, scented varieties
Pansies
Valerian
Madonna lilies
Sweet Williams
Alchemilla mollis
Digitalis
Bulbs: tulips, narcissus, bluebells, muscari
Container plants requiring shelter in the winter such as some fuchsias and pelargoniums

Contemporary

The well-known, widely travelled John Brookes is recognized as being at the forefront of contemporary garden design. When looking at his gardens it is strikingly obvious that his use of hard landscaping is beautiful in the way that it exhibits the chosen material to the best of its potential, and the fusion between hard landscaping and surrounding environment is seamless.

Characteristics
- Less is more: the dominant element of a contemporary garden is the hard landscaping rather than the planting.
- Strong architectural use of foliage shape.
- Colour contrasts.
- Use of several focal point plants, rather than one or two.
- Strong use of form.
- The planting is often conspicuous by its absence. In other words, there is very little of it. On occasions a specific plant group may be

selected, such as sedum, and only that plant group used; or only one variety of plant is used.
- Grass is seen as a 'plant' and used as such. For example, the design may have a beautiful sinuous limestone pathway, flanked on either side by lawns. In this instance the green of the grass is seen as planting, whereas in a traditional-style garden the path is highly likely to be flanked by a herbaceous border on both sides.

Contemporary style plants
Phormiums
Cordylines
Yuccas
Sedums
Tree ferns
Fatsia japonica
Ophiopogon planiscapus 'Nigrescens'
Grass

Architectural

Characteristics
- Strong form and movement.
- The movement is seen in the shape of the plant; for example, the strong, upright, sword-like growth habit of the *Phormium tenax* species is not dissimilar in shape to a firework.

A more comprehensive list of architectural plants can be found in the plant library in Chapter 5.

Some architectural style plants
Phormiums
Cordylines
Cardoon
Yucca gloriosa

Chinese and Japanese

Chinese characteristics
- Very restrained plant palette.
- Highly ordered, meticulous in its detail and use of materials.
- Use of rocks.

- The essence of Chinese garden style is based upon two spiritual belief systems – Confucianism and Taoism. Confucianism teaches order and duty; Taoism simplicity and restraint. A Chinese style garden is very much an outward expression of a culture that embraces these spiritual beliefs and it gives deep insight into the religious culture of these two age-old religions. Every element in a Chinese garden has a meaning – even the rocks. The plant palette is kept to a minimum to accentuate the hard landscaping and structures.

Chinese style plants
Pinus
Magnolias
Rhododendrons
Dwarf Azaleas
Acer trees
Moss
Bamboos
Camellias

Japanese dry garden characteristics
- No plants at all except perhaps for the minimal use of moss by the edge of a small pool or at the base of a rock.
- The Japanese dry garden is, as it says, a dry garden of raked gravel with fourteen carefully placed rocks.
- It is a garden intended for deep meditation and contemplation, hence the absence of any plants and colour, which according to the Zen monks who pioneered this type of garden, would be a distraction.

Gravel garden planting style.

Scree or gravel

Characteristics
- Drought-tolerant plants.
- Plants in random-shaped and smaller, manageable groups.
- Sense of informality.
- Planting can be walked through and around.
- Mulched with fine gravel which serves to reduce surface evaporation from the soil and so retain moisture. The gravel also serves to provide a hard-wearing surface for walking around the garden, but with no defined pathway.

Scree or gravel style plants
Grasses
Drought-tolerant herbaceous perennials such as Echinacea, Kniphofia, *Lychnis coronaria*, Achillea, *Acaena* 'Blue Haze', Agapanthus, Verbena genus, Verbascums, Sedums, *Stachys byzantina* 'Big Ears', Potentilla, Penstemon, Nepeta, Linum, Limonium, Eryngium.
Alliums
Cistus genus
Perennial geraniums
Cordylines
Yucca

The gravel garden style is particularly appropriate for use in today's unpredictable weather patterns. In a prolonged period of hot, dry summer weather, the tough nature of the plants, together with the gravel mulch, will considerably increase the length of time for which the garden looks colourful and healthy. The nature of the plants – the high density of seed-producing herbaceous perennials and grasses – is a highly valuable resource as food for wildlife; and their low maintenance requirements make this type of garden very desirable for the busy lifestyle of many people in today's society.

Prairie

Characteristics
- Low usage of shrubs.

- Late colour: the majority of prairie species flower in late summer to early autumn, at a time which is often a dull season in many gardens.
- An extended season of interest is provided by the use of some shrubs and conifers in combination with the herbaceous prairie planting.
- Diverse in both its species and visual content.

Prairie plants
Echinacea purpurea
Coreopsis grandiflora
Monarda fistulosa
Hemerocallis lilioasphodelus
Anaphalis margaritacea
Nepeta racemosa 'Superba'
Verbascum chaixii
Dianthus carthusianorum
Astilbe chinensis var. pumila
Deschampsia cespitosa
Iris unguicularis
Verbena hastate
Salvia pratensis
Stipa gigantea
Geranium 'Johnson's Blue'

Plants providing an extended season of interest
Albertiana conica
Alliums for seedhead interest
Caryopteris 'Grand Bleu'
Ceratostigma willmottianum
Chamaecyparis lawsoniana 'Minima Aurea'
Cistus 'Grayswood Pink'
Cistus 'Peggy Sammons'
Cistus 'Silver Pink'
Convolvulus cneorum
Cordyline australis
Cornus alba sibirica
Corokia macrocarpa 'Red Wonder'
Cryptomeria japonica 'Sekkan-sugi'
Cupressus sempervirens
Erysium 'Bowles' Mauve'
Foeniculum vulgare 'Purpureum'
Fuchsia 'Mrs Popple'
Juniperus communis 'Compressa'

A beautiful example of prairie-style planting at Knoll Gardens.

Juniperus communis 'Gold Cone'
Juniperus communis 'Green Carpet'
Juniperus horizontalis 'Glauca'
Juniperus horizontalis 'Lime Glow'
Juniperus scopulorum 'Blue Arrow'
Magnolia stellata
Origanum vulgare 'Aurea'
Picea glauca 'Albertiana Globe'
Pinus mugo 'Gnom'
Taxus baccata 'Fastigiata'
Thuja orientalis 'Aurea Nana'

Most of the plants suggested to extend the season of interest are evergreen and/or provide strong form, a second framework that takes over through the winter months in a prairie style garden.

Colour schemed

This is not a conventional planting style; however, I have included it in this category because when a planting scheme is colour schemed/coordinated it results in a highly stylized effect.

A specific planting style can be reminiscent of any era in history; it will use plants that are of that era, or recent varieties planted in an appropriate way. I have focused on planting styles because this book is about planting design; however, when creating a specific garden style, attention will also need to be paid to the hard landscaping elements of the era to gain the full effect.

5 PLANT SHAPES

Unfortunately, there is very little published information to be found regarding the use of plant shapes as a planting design tool. What little is to be found is very heavy on its use of text; or if it does use drawn shapes, it fails to explore the subject to its maximum potential. Hence the birth and evolution of this book.

So far we have looked in Chapter 1 at the theory of planting design and introduced you to a whole new perspective on planting a garden; in Chapter 2 on plant use we considered and explored 'how' plants can be used in the garden; planting design, in Chapter 3, focused on garden 'aesthetics' – how a planting scheme looks – rather than on the mechanics of which soil, which aspect, and so on. Then Chapter 4 explored and described the various component parts of particular garden styles. With all of that supporting information and theory, we can now focus on the subject matter at the heart of the book: plant shapes.

When looking at a border or bed, most gardeners, enthusiasts and students see a collection of plants, but this is just the tip of the iceberg! The 'plant collection' is often defined and described by colour: 'Ooh isn't that blue lovely', or 'That red is too strong and clashes with the yellow', are the type of descriptive comments commonly heard. This is, of course, because we cannot all know all of the plants' names, but also because we use vision to vividly describe something. Less often, plants that have a strong shape are singled out: 'Isn't that a lovely cone-shaped conifer', or 'I really like that clipped, ball-shape plant'. Our attention is taken by the colours and the brain becomes busy interpreting all the information, and yet plant shapes are the very backbone of a successful planting scheme.

It is not until the less obvious aspects of plants are recognized, in terms of their 'role and effect' within a scheme, that the shape of a plant becomes more apparent and acknowledged as providing the effect that it does. Occasionally, we may dislike a planting scheme and it is then, in the process of assessing why we don't like it, dividing it into its component parts and discovering aspects of plants which previously had gone unrecognized, that the substance behind the mask is discovered. Interestingly enough, imbalance and disparity in a planting scheme are often due to the incorrect use of a strong plant shape, when its dominance tips the scales rather than balancing them.

THE NINE PLANT SHAPES

1. Ball, sphere or globe.
2. Architectural/spiky.
3. Mound/dome – large, medium and small.
4. Pillar/column – tall, medium and small.
5. Triangle/cone – large, medium and small.
6. Trapezium/waterfall/fan.
7. Oblong/rectangle.
8. Random/irregular.
9. Prostrate.

OPPOSITE: **Allium christopherii.**
(Photo: Rhoda Nottridge)

There are nine plant shapes; each shape is described here for its use and effect, and supported by a plant library, images and technical information. In the plant library, height (H) and width (W) are given for each plant.

BALL/SPHERE/GLOBE

Role and effect

This shape stops the eye and thereby creates a full stop at either the end of a border or within the border, holding the viewer's interest. If particular attention is required to be paid to a special plant or sculpture in the middle of a border, placing a 'ball' shape in front of the object will cause the eye to stop at the ball shape and take in the focal point behind it.

Most ball/sphere shapes are found as clipped evergreens, usually box; however, the ball/sphere shape can be sourced as a half or full standard, with the ball on top of a slim trunk being nearer to eye level and appearing almost to float above

Ball/sphere/globe.

other planting. Clipped laurel, otherwise known as bay trees, are the favoured genus, although today other species are available such as *Photinia* and *Viburnum*.

Other species, as listed in the plant section below, either have a natural growth habit towards the spherical, or lend themselves and respond very well to being clipped.

All provide permanent form, a sense of formality and a focal point, and rhythm if several are planted in a row or group.

Lavandula angustifolia 'Munstead' showing its natural globe shape.

Lavandula angustifolia 'Munstead' and Lavandula stoechas 'Papillon'

Soil: Well drained.
Aspect: Full sun.
Growth habit: H 45cm × W 60–70cm.
Season of interest: Late spring/early summer flower, year-round silver and green foliage.

Lavendula stoechas 'Papillon'.

Design use: Clipped dwarf hedging, permanent edging, permanent form, aromatic flower and foliage, attracts bees.

Buxus sempervirens (Shrub)

Soil: Moisture retentive, but not wet in the winter.
Aspect: Partial shade – scorches in full sun.
Growth habit: Up to H 70cm × W 50cm if left unclipped.
Season of interest: Small white/pale green flowers in spring, year-round evergreen form – particularly if clipped into a shape.
Design use: Clipped dwarf hedging, topiary globe, spiral and cone shapes, adds a sense of formality to a planting scheme.

Santolina chamaecyparissus (Sub shrub)

Soil: Dry, free draining.
Aspect: Full sun.
Growth habit: H 60cm × W 70cm.

Buxus sempervirens spheres, their perfectly clipped shape outlined against the pale gravel.

Santolina chamaecyparissus.

Season of interest: Late spring and early summer.
Design use: Late spring/early summer colour.
Eye-catching purple, globe-shaped flower heads –
fantastic planted in large groups. Exquisite seed
heads for autumn/winter interest.

Laurus nobilis (Standard clipped bay tree)

Soil: Moist, well-drained soil.
Aspect: Full sun/partial shade.

Season of interest: Yellow, button-like summer
flowers, year-round silver foliage.
Design use: Permanent form, aromatic foliage,
summer flower, good in gravel garden, good
for dwarf hedging.

Abies balsamea 'Nana' (Conifer)

Soil: Moist but well drained, neutral to slightly
acid soil.
Aspect: Full sun, shelter from cold winds.
Growth habit: Very slow growing, will reach up
to H 30–40cm × W 40–50cm in ten years.
Season of interest: Year-round, evergreen.
Design use: Permanent form and texture, focal
point plant, conifer and heather garden, gravel
garden.

Allium christophii, Allium hollandicum 'Purple Sensation' (Bulb)

Soil: Well drained, no wet in winter as it rots the
bulb.
Aspect: Full sun.
Growth habit: H 40–50cm.

Allium christophii.

Allium hollandicum **'Purple Sensation'**.

Tsuga canadensis 'Jeddeloh' (Hemlock)

Soil: Humus rich, moist, well drained. Acid to slightly alkaline.
Aspect: Full sun/partial shade.
Growth habit: Up to H 1.5m × W 2m.
Season of interest: Year-round evergreen permanent form.
Design use: Interesting weeping growth habit, bright green leaves darkening as they age, conifer and heather garden, focal point plant.

Picea pungens 'Globosa' (Spruce)

Soil: Deep, moist but well drained soil. Neutral to acid.
Aspect: Full sun.
Growth habit: Slow growing. Round ball shape up to W 40–50cm in ten years.
Season of interest: Year-round evergreen permanent form.
Design use: Focal point plant, to add texture, interesting growth habit.

Growth habit: Can be grown as large shrub or clipped to shape.
Season of interest: Year-round evergreen permanent form.
Design use: To add height and formality, standards mark entrance if planted either side of pathway. Add rhythm if several planted in a row.

Hard landscaping can also be used to replicate the plant forms, for example in garden ornaments such as the sandstone balls illustrated overleaf.

Laurus nobilis – a clipped, globe-shaped standard bay tree.

Picea pungens 'Globosa'.

Features such as these sandstone balls can be used to complement the plant shapes.

It is interesting to note that the most popular of these are the cordyline, palm and phormium families, which, coming from hotter climes, remind us of a warmer environment.

Phormium tenax

Soil: Moist, well drained.
Aspect: Full sun.
Growth habit: Up to H 4m × W 2m.
Season of interest: Year-round.
Design use: Adds a contemporary feel, lifts a border/scheme, many colour variations available. Evergreen/seasonal interest. Unusual flower spikes. Exotic scheme. Focal point plant.

ARCHITECTURAL/SPIKY

Role and effect

The architectural, spiky shape adds drama. The strong upward growth habit of pointed leaves leads the eye skyward, like the explosion of a firework. Due to their dramatic nature, they demand attention and provide a very strong focal point in a border. Most of these plants are evergreen, which makes this a permanent effect.

Phormium tenax.

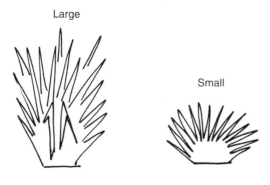

Large

Small

Architectural/spiky/firework.

Cordyline australis (Cabbage palm)

Soil: Well drained.
Aspect: Full sun.
Growth habit: H 3–10m, forms a trunk as lower leaves are removed.
Season of interest: Year-round.
Design use: 'Firework' effect at ground level when first planted. Adds contemporary feel to scheme. Evergreen. Exotic scheme. Focal point plant.

Trachycarpus fortunei.

Iris sibirica

Soil: Damp soil, but not clay.
Aspect: Full sun/partial shade.
Growth habit: H 50–120cm. Clump forming.
Season of interest: Early summer, bright intense blue flowers. Alba bears white flowers.
Design use: Early summer colour, poolside planting, foliage provides smaller architectural effect.

Cordyline australis.

Trachycarpus fortunei

Soil: Well drained, fertile.
Aspect: Full sun/light dappled shade.
Growth habit: Relatively slow growing but can become a tree in twenty years plus. Initially approx. H 60–80cm × W 70–80cm.
Season of interest: Year-round.
Design use: Interesting leaf formation. Forms trunk. Exotic scheme. Adds contemporary feel. Focal point plant.

The spiky foliage of *Iris sibirica*.

Crocosmia × *crocosmiiflora* (Montbretia, bulb)

Soil: Humus rich, moist but well drained soil.
Aspect: Sun/partial shade.
Growth habit: H 60cm × each bulb approx. W 8cm. Clump forming.
Season of interest: Summer/autumn flowering.
Design use: Bright orange flowers, long flowering season, tough plant, interesting seed heads, Bright green, architectural foliage at lower height. Many variations of yellows, oranges and reds available in this family.

Kniphofia uvaria 'Nobilis'.

Crocosmia 'Star of the East'.

Kniphofia uvaria 'Nobilis' (Herbaceous perennial)

Soil: Humus rich, moist, well drained soil.
Aspect: Full sun/partial shade.
Growth habit: H 1.2m × W 60cm.
Season of interest: Year-round interest from foliage, summer/autumn flower.
Design use: Evergreen foliage, bright orange flowers that fade to yellow.
Mid-height colour in a border. Many variations of yellows, lemon to pale greens, and oranges available in this family.

Yucca gloriosa

Soil: Well drained.
Aspect: Full sun.
Growth habit: Slow growing.
Season of interest: Year-round.
Design use: Striking architectural shape, variegated varieties available, focal point plant, forms trunk eventually.

Yucca gloriosa.

Verbascum olympicum (Mullein, herbaceous perennial)

Soil: Alkaline, poor, well drained.
Aspect: Full sun.
Growth habit: Very upright. Up to H 2m × W 60cm.
Season of interest: Summer into autumn flower.
Design use: Grey, furry, textural foliage, pale yellow flowers in spikelets branching from main stem. Tall plant, height at rear of border. Focal point plant.

Sisyrinchium striatum (Iridaceae)

Soil: Poor to moderately fertile, well drained, neutral to slightly alkaline.
Aspect: Full sun. Protect from excessive wet in the winter.
Growth habit: Up to H 60cm × W 25cm. Clump forming.
Season of interest: Year-round.
Design use: Year-round evergreen foliage, pale yellow summer flower, interesting seed heads, architectural foliage at front of border, good gravel garden plant.

Sisyrinchium striatum.

Angelica archangelica

Soil: Fertile, moist, loamy, well drained.
Aspect: Full sun.
Growth habit: Up to H 2m × W 1.8m.
Season of interest: Summer and autumn.
Design use: Focal point plant, striking foliage and flower heads that provide winter interest; however, it dies after flowering, but if spent flowers are removed before setting seed it may flower for a second year.

The large architectural flower heads and foliage of *Angelica archangelica*.

Cyperus papyrus

Soil: Damp soil.
Aspect: Sun/partial shade.
Growth habit: H 60–90cm × W 45cm.
Season of interest: Summer.
Design use: Poolside planting. Damp area in a garden. Textural seed heads and foliage. May be killed by extreme winter cold.

Cyperus papyrus.

Eryngium giganteum
(Herbaceous perennial)

Soil: Dry, well drained, protect from winter wet.
Aspect: Full sun.
Growth habit: H 90cm × W 30cm.
Season of interest: Year-round foliage interest, summer thistle-like flowers.
Design use: Striking grey/green foliage colour. Spiky, silver thistle-like flowers.
Good in gravel garden, mid-border height.

MOUND/DOME

Role and effect

The dome/mound shaped plant has the effect of 'anchoring' the planting scheme wherever it is positioned. Dome/mound shaped plants are to be found in three sizes, large, medium and small, and are used in multiples throughout a planted area (for example, a large mound shaped shrub at the rear planted with three medium mounds mid-border and three small mound shaped plants at the front).

The strong architectural spike shape is softened by having mound shaped plants next to or near to them.

This shape is commonly found in the shrub, herbaceous perennial and small shrub groups, and will provide a mixture of deciduous and evergreen plants.

Sedum spectabile 'Brilliant'
(Hardy succulent)

Soil: Free draining to dry.
Aspect: Full sun.
Growth habit: Upright, clump forming. H approx. 22cm; W narrow at base, crown approx. 60cm.
Season of interest: Early summer for foliage, autumn until first frosts for flower colour, through winter for seed head interest.
Design use: Succulent – foliage has smooth textured, fat pale green leaves. Dry gravel garden

The silver architectural flower heads of *Eryngium giganteum* contrasted with the brightly-coloured *Alstroemeria*.

Sedum spectabile 'Brilliant'.

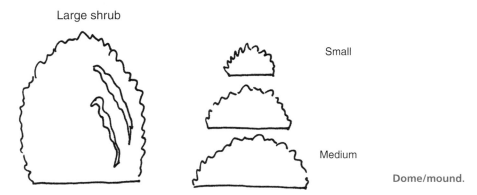

Large shrub

Small

Medium

Dome/mound.

for summer, autumn and winter interest. To attract butterflies and birds. Low maintenance.

Buxus sempervirens

Soil: Most garden soils, but will not tolerate extreme dry in the summer months.

Aspect: Full to partial sun.
Growth habit: Small shrub. H 60–90cm × W 60–75cm.
Season of interest: Year-round; evergreen.
Design use: Small evergreen shrub, responds well to clipping, can be used for topiary or dwarf hedging.

A collection of assorted-sized mounds of *Buxus sempervirens*.

Eragrostis curvula (Grass)

Soil: Moist but free draining.
Aspect: Full sun, will also thrive in morning sun only.
Growth habit: Clump forming. Fine, arching leaves. H 60–70cm × W 80cm–1m.
Season of interest: Summer for foliage, late summer for seed head interest.
Design use: Good tough plant. Excellent in low maintenance scheme. Adds movement. Lovely arching leaves and delicate flower in late summer. Good for grasses scheme and combining with herbaceous perennials.

Nepeta 'Walker's Low' (Hardy perennial)

Soil: Most soils, but well drained.
Aspect: Full sun.
Growth habit: Clump forming, H approx. 45–50cm × W 45–50cm.
Season of interest: Early to late summer.
Design use: Evergreen/grey, aromatic foliage at low level. Low maintenance. Gravel garden, hot sunny border, striking sky blue flowers.

Erysium 'Bowles' Mauve' (Sub shrub, evergreen perennial)

Soil: Variable, but not heavy clay.
Aspect: Full sun to partial shade.
Growth habit: H 45–50cm × W 45–50cm.
Season of interest: Year-round evergreen/grey foliage. Intense lilac flowers from April to first frosts.
Design use: Year-round foliage, long flowering season, gravel garden, sunny border. Low maintenance.

Hosta fortunei 'Albo Picta' (Hardy herbaceous perennial)

Soil: Moist, will also thrive in wet clay soils.
Aspect: Full sun to partial shade.
Growth habit: Clump forming, H 20–30cm × W 30–40cm.
Season of interest: Spring through summer until autumn.
Design use: A wide variety of foliage colour available, from glossy greens, blue and lime greens to variegated cream/green, yellow/green, white/ green. Summer flower spikes of trumpet-shaped lavender or white flowers. Fantastic for clay soils, anywhere that remains damp. Look

Eragrostis curvula.

Nepeta 'Walker's Low' as permanent path edging, with its pale blue flowers through summer and ever-grey foliage through winter.

wonderful grown in pots – add water gel crystals to retain moisture.

Carex testacea (Hardy evergreen grass)

Soil: Most soils, well drained.
Aspect: Full sun to partial shade.
Growth habit: Small, clump forming. H 30cm × W 20–30cm.
Season of interest: Year-round.

Design use: Small bronze/green grass which is a superb colour contrast with deep lilacs, purples and oranges. Gravel garden, front of border, seasonal interest.

Hosta fortunei 'Albo Picta'.

Carex testacea.

Phormium 'Yellow Wave' (Hardy evergreen perennial)

Soil: Fertile, moist, well drained.
Aspect: Full sun.
Growth habit: Clumps of large, linear, strap-like leaves. *Tenax* group – up to H 1.5–1.8m × approx. W 1.5m. *Cookianum* group – up to H 1–1.2m × W 1–1.5m.
Season of interest: Year-round.
Design use: Evergreen. Strong, architectural shape. Focal point plant. Gravel garden. Low maintenance. Wide variety of cultivars available with many variegations of cream/greens, yellow/greens, pink/greens and flat green, black/purple and bronze foliage colours. Two growth habits available – the *Tenax* group, strong, upright; and the *Cookianum* group, softer, arching. Add a contemporary sense to a border.

TALL MOUND/DOME

Role and effect

Used towards the back of a border, a larger dome/mound shaped plant 'anchors' the planting at the back of the scheme, wherever it is positioned. Large deciduous dome/mound shaped shrubs provide skeletal interest in the winter, and some increase their interest by producing flowers, often heavily scented, on bare stems. Large evergreen dome/mound shaped shrubs provide a permanant backdrop to plants at the front of the border.

Euphorbia characias subsp. wulfenii 'John Tomlinson' (Milkweed or spurge, hardy perennial)

Soil: Well drained but moist.
Aspect: Sun/partial shade.
Growth habit: H and W up to 1.2m. Clump forming.
Season of interest: Early spring to early summer.
Design use: Strong upright growth habit, with large, almost spherical green flower heads known as 'cyathia'.

Euphorbia carachias subsp. *wulfenii* 'John Tomlinson'.

Hydrangea macrophylla (Common hydrangea, shrub)

Soil: Moist, well drained, moderately fertile.
Aspect: Sun/partial shade.
Growth habit: Large rounded shrub. Up to H 1.5m × W 1.2m.
Season of interest: Middle to late summer for flower, large, glossy green foliage prior to and after flowering until first frosts.
Design use: Many flower colours available, long flowering season, large, spherical flower heads add visual interest even when dead – often used by florists. Easy to grow and maintain.

Hydrangea macrophylla **with its mound-shaped flower heads and overall mounded growth habit.**

Cornus genus (Dogwood, shrub)

Soil: Prefer moist soil, will tolerate quite wet soil.

Aspect: Sun/partial shade.

Growth habit: Medium to large rounded shrub. H and W up to 1.8m for large varieties and H and W 1m for smaller varieties.

Season of interest: Year-round – deciduous but provide coloured stems for autumn/winter interest. Spring – white flower heads. Variety of foliage and stem colours available.

Design use: Winter stem interest looks fantastic when planted in groups. Recommended varieties: *Cornus alba* 'Elegantissima' – red stems, variegated foliage; *Cornus alba sibirica* – red stems, red autumn foliage colour; *Cornus stolonifera* 'Flaviramea' – lime green stems; *Cornus alba* 'Kesselringii' – dark black/purple stems, red and purple autumn foliage colour.

The vivid red stems of *Cornus alba sibirica*.

Abies nordmanniana 'Golden Spreader' (Conifer)

Soil: Moist to well drained, neutral to slightly acid soil.

Aspect: Full sun, shelter from cold winds.

Growth habit: Slow growing, up to H 1m × W 1.5m.

Season of interest: Evergreen, year-round seasonal interest.

Design use: Use in herbaceous border for evergreen form. Golden colour throughout year, good planted with heathers and ferns.

Abies nordmanniana 'Golden Spreader'.

Pinus mugo 'Gnom' (Dwarf mountain pine)

Soil: Well drained, moist soil.

Aspect: Full sun to partial shade.

Growth habit: H 45– 47cm × W 90cm.

Season of interest: Evergreen year-round seasonal interest, strong form.

Design use: Forms a dense, globular, dark green mound; this is sometimes considered the best dwarf mugo; 'Gnom' tends to have a flat top.

Pinus mugo 'Gnom'.

Spiraea 'Arguta' (Bridal wreath, shrub)

Soil: Well drained, moist, fertile.
Aspect: Full sun.
Growth habit: Rounded shrub with arching branches. Up to H 2m and W 2m.
Season of interest: Early spring – the branches are smothered in fresh green foliage and small white flowers.
Design use: Mixed border, towards the rear.

PILLAR/COLUMN

Role and effect

The pillar/column shape is very elegant, with the effect of narrow height. A single pillar/column acts as an exclamation mark, causing the eye to stop and focus; several used in a row will create strong, dynamic rhythm, and underplanted with grass or a hard surface can be a high impact planting scheme in their own right.

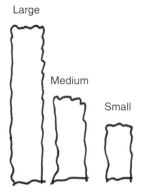

Pillar/column.

Plants in this group can be categorized into tall, medium and low pillar/column shape plants.

Early-flowering *Spiraea* 'Arguta' with spring bulbs.

They are mostly small trees and evergreens. Very few, if any, herbaceous perennials have a pillar/column shape growth habit.

TALL PILLAR/COLUMN SHAPE PLANTS

Taxus baccata 'Fastigiata' (Irish yew, Florence court yew; tree)

Soil: Well drained/light, chalky/alkaline, moist, sandy.
Aspect: Full sun.
Growth habit: H 3m × up to W 1.50m.
Season of interest: Dark evergreen year-round. Yellow flowers in spring, red fruits in autumn.
Design use: Evergreen. Its very dense habit makes it particularly useful as a hedging plant, or as a striking specimen plant. It is a slow-growing yew which naturally makes a good shape without any clipping or trimming. It forms a tall, upright-growing tree with a columnar habit and can be used to add height and winter structure to the garden. It is one of the best garden yews, as it will take many years to outgrow its position.
Caution: Most parts, especially the seeds, are highly toxic if eaten.

Amelanchier alnifolia 'Obelisk' (Tree)

Soil: Any soil type.
Aspect: It will thrive in any position.

ABOVE: *Amelanchier alnifolia* 'Obelisk'.

BELOW: **Using a column shape:** *Taxus baccata* 'fastigiata' **echoing uprights of the structure.**

Growth habit: After five years it will reach approx. H 3–4m × W 50–60cm.

Season of interest: Year-round. Attractive foliage of dark green, almost circular leaves which change to yellow in the autumn. During late April/early May the stems are covered in white flowers, sometimes turning into edible berries in autumn. Attractive, skeletal shape during the winter when the branches are bare. In a small garden this small tree is particularly useful as it gives more than one season of interest.

Design use: Small, low maintenance tree – no need to prune, as it forms a compact shape by itself, therefore will not outgrow its space. *Amelanchier alnifolia* 'Obelisk' is a magnificent small deciduous tree with an upright, slender shape, allowing you the opportunity to give your garden some 'height interest' without it taking over! It looks good as part of a border display or as a specimen plant in a lawn or gravel bed.

Prunus serrulata 'Amanogawa' (Tree)

Soil: Moderately moist.
Aspect: Full sun.
Growth habit: Up to H 6m × W 2m.
Season of interest: Spring and winter.
Design use: Tall, columnar, skeletal shape through winter. Pink or white spring flower. Good for small gardens or where space will only allow for a narrow tree. Japanese style garden.

MEDIUM PILLAR/COLUMN SHAPE PLANTS

Foeniculum vulgare 'Purpureum' (Fennel; herb)

Soil: Well drained/light, dry, sandy.
Aspect: Full sun.
Growth habit: Upright, spreading. H 80cm–1m × W 45cm.
Season of interest: Summer.
Design use: Hardy, deciduous. Terrific bronze, purple aromatic (aniseed) scented foliage in summer. Great attraction for butterflies and beneficial insects. The licorice-flavoured leaves

Foeniculum vulgare 'Purpureum'.

and seeds are used in many different recipes. Umbels of yellow flowers in summer.

Helianthus 'Multiflorus' (Hardy herbaceous perennial)

Soil: Alkaline, moist, rich and well drained soil.
Aspect: Full sun.
Growth habit: Tall clump. H 2m × W 1m.
Season of interest: Summer/autumn.
Design use: A hardy herbaceous perennial with a long flowering period. Vigorous – needs plenty of room towards the back of the border. Its shape is described as upright. Dark green foliage. Produces flowers during summer/autumn that are daisy-shaped and yellow in colour. This plant is likely to need staking. It is susceptible to, and should be protected from, slugs and snails and mildew.

Helianthus multiflorus.

Juniper communis 'Gold Cone'.

SMALL PILLAR/COLUMN SHAPE PLANTS

Juniperus communis 'Gold Cone' (Conifer)

Soil: Well drained soil.
Aspect: Full sun/dappled shade.
Growth habit: Upright. Very slow growing: H 0.5–6m × W 20cm–1 or 2m in 20 years.
Season of interest: Year-round.
Design use: Small, upright evergreen column. Very slow growing, safe to use in small gardens. Ideal for rockery planting and front of gravel garden. Can be used as an alternative to *Cupressus sempervirens*, which is faster growing. Low maintenance.

TRIANGLE/CONE

Role and effect

The triangle/cone shape is very striking; it adds height, which is anchored by the wider base, and the eye is taken upwards from the base to an

Taxus baccata 'Fastigiata' (small pillar).

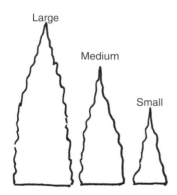

Triangle/cone.

should be pruned back or tied in during the winter months – the weight of snow will cause them to protrude and spoil the overall shape of the tree.

Cupressus sempervirens **accentuating the rectangular pool with height.**

almost pointed top. The shape can be a focal point plant, particularly when an evergreen is used, and also adds a sense of formality. The slender *Cupressus sempivirens* is not dissimilar to a soldier on parade!

In very old formal gardens, you can see the fun that was had by mixing a variety of evergreens, some clipped into shape and some developing their distinctive natural shape. They almost look like chess pieces.

The positioning of this shape is dependent upon the ultimate size of the chosen species. Towards the rear is ideal for larger evergreens; smaller species can be positioned towards the front of the border.

Cupressus sempervirens (Conifer)

Soil: Well drained.
Aspect: Full sun. Shelter from strong winds.
Growth habit: Upright. H 4–5m in ten years. W up to 1.5m, stays very narrow at the base.
Season of interest: Year-round.
Design use: Strong, narrow, evergreen height. Creates an 'exclamation mark' in a border. Ideal for small gardens as stays very narrow and will not swamp a border as other conifers have a tendency to do. Adds a sense of formality, and a Mediterranean feel to the planting. Needs light clipping to keep shape and any branches which are 'leaning away' from the main framework

Juniperus scopulorum 'Skyrocket' (Conifer)

Soil: Well drained.
Aspect: Full sun/dappled shade.
Growth habit: Upright. H approx. 6m in ten years; W 1–2m, stays very narrow at the base.
Season of interest: Year-round.
Design use: Strong, blue-grey evergreen which adds permanent height. Loose growth habit.
Good contrast foliage colour. Good for small gardens.

Cryptomeria japonica 'Sekkan-sugi' (Conifer)

Soil: Well drained – does especially well in a fertile, humus-rich soil.
Aspect: Full sun/partial shade.
Growth habit: Moderately slow growing. H approx. 3–5m × W up to 2m in ten years.
Season of interest: Year-round, but particularly interesting colour change from creamy yellow to almost white in winter.

Juniperus scopulorum 'Skyrocket'.

ABOVE: *Cryptomeria japonica* 'Sekkan-sugi'.

BELOW: *Pinus parviflora* 'Templehof'.

Design use: A soft, creamy yellow conifer, with a pendant growth habit. Unusual needle formation. Adds a splash of 'light' to a border, with its contrasting, creamy yellow colour.

Pinus parviflora 'Templehof' (Conifer)

Soil: Well drained.
Aspect: Full sun.
Growth habit: Relatively slow growing. H 1–2m, W approx. 1m in ten years.
Season of interest: Year-round.
Design use: One of the best blue pinus species. Long needles in groups of five around the stem which make it an interesting pine to look at closely, in conjunction with its overall interesting shape. Good for small gardens. In a Japanese garden the oriental sense is strengthened by using the plant. Looks great planted in gravel as part of a group or as a focal point plant.

Thuja occidentalis 'Smaragd' (Conifer)

Soil: Deep, moist, well drained soil.
Aspect: Full sun, shelter from cold winds.
Growth habit: H approx. 2–3m × W at base 60–70cm in ten years.
Season of interest: Year-round.
Design use: Strong, narrow, evergreen cone/triangle. Good conifer for small gardens and spaces as maintains a narrow base.

Picea glauca var. albertiana 'Conica' (Conifer)

Soil: Deep, moist, neutral to acid soil.
Aspect: Full sun.
Growth habit: H 90–120cm × W 45–60cm at base.
Season of interest: Year-round. Particularly in spring as develops two small brown buds at end of each shoot, these burst open with new, bright green foliage, which transforms the plant.

Design use: Conifer garden, excellent for topiary, good small- to medium-sized cone/triangle shape in a border.

Chamaecyparis thyoides 'Top Point' (Conifer)

Soil: Moist to wet. Neutral to alkaline.
Aspect: Sun/partial shade.
Growth habit: Mature in approx. 10 years at H 1.2m × W 20–30cm at base.
Season of interest: Year-round. Evergreen. Bright green little cone/triangle of juvenile foliage with an interesting two texture effect.
Design use: Conifer garden; small triangle/cone in a border; could be used in Japanese/Chinese style garden.

Thuja occidentalis 'Smaragd'.

Picea glauca var. *albertiana* 'Conica'.

Chamaecyparis thyoides 'Top Point'.

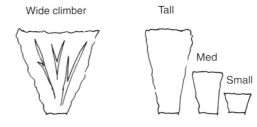

Fan/waterfall/trapezium.

TRAPEZIUM/FAN AND WATERFALL

Role and effect

This shape adds both height and width at height when used at the back of a border, plant species of choice being climbers such as clematis, honeysuckle, jasmine, *Hydrangea petiolaris* (climbing hydrangea) and ivy.

Other plants that provide this effect are *Phyllostachys* (bamboo), which has a strong fan shape and is free standing, and can therefore be used at the rear of a border, in the middle section or as a focal point. Please note when selecting bamboo that it can be very invasive, so always select the clump-forming varieties (see the plant library) that stay narrow at the base.

This shape can be seen in three sizes: large (mostly climbers and bamboo), medium, and small (mostly the herbaceous group). The fan shape, again, has a strong upward movement, but also provides a horizontal line and width across the top of the plant which is above ground level.

TALL TRAPEZIUM/FAN SHAPED PLANTS

Phyllostachys nigra (Black bamboo)

Soil: Fertile, humus rich, moist soil – not boggy.
Aspect: Full sun/dappled shade.
Growth habit: H 3–5m; W narrow clump at the base 50cm up to 1.5–2m in approx. twenty years.
Season of interest: Year-round evergreen.
Design use: Strong, upright fan shape. Good for evergreen screening, waterside planting if at least 1m away. Use in Japanese/Chinese garden style. Lovely movement and rustling sound in the wind.

Leycesteria Formosa (Shrub)

Soil: Good soil, well drained.
Aspect: Full sun/partial shade.
Growth habit: Up to H 2m × W 1.5m.
Season of interest: Year-round. Bright green cane-like stems are of interest in the winter.

Leycesteria formosa.

Design use: Good plant for rear of border, lovely heart shaped green foliage, with bunches of white flowers underneath claret red bracts. When flowers die, they form pea-sized shiny black berries. Tough plant that is of year-round interest.

Clematis (Climber)

Soil: Well drained, moist at the roots.
Aspect: Full sun, roots must be shaded.
Growth habit: H varies with the variety but most will grow in excess of 2m. W narrow at the base, approx. 40cm wider at the top.
Season of interest: There are clematis varieties for all seasons.
Design use: Good for disguising fences and bringing added vertical colour into the garden. Can be grown as focal point plant on an obelisk, pergola or archway. Can be grown through trees/large shrubs.

ABOVE: *Clematis* 'Madame Julia Correvon' and 'Perle d'Azur'.

BELOW: Clematis – a natural fan shape.

Cercis canadensis 'Forest Pansy' (Shrub)

Soil: Fertile. Well drained.
Aspect: Full sun/dappled shade.
Growth habit: Can become tree-like in size in many years, but can be pruned to required size.
Season of interest: Spring through to autumn.
Design use: Produces tiny, bright pink flowers on bare stems in spring. Leaves are of particular interest being large, deep red, and heart shaped. Lovely open growth habit. Wonderful autumn foliage colour.

Stipa gigantea (Grass)

Soil: Medium to light, well drained soil.
Aspect: Full sun.
Growth habit: Up to H 2m × W 1m at the base, wider at the top.
Season of interest: Year-round.
Design use: Good in gravel garden or as a specimen focal point plant in a herbaceous border. Beautiful delicate, golden grass flowers in spring, maturing into oat-like seeds that dance at the top of long elegant stems. Birds love this plant.

Cercis canadensis 'Forest Pansy'.

Stipa gigantea.

Miscanthus sacchariflorus (Grass)

Soil: Will tolerate most soils but best in a moist, well drained soil. Does not like excessive winter wet.
Aspect: Full sun.
Growth habit: Up to H 2–2.5m × W 60cm at base, 1–1.4m at the top.
Season of interest: Year-round.
Design use: Robust, tall grass which looks good in a gravel garden, herbaceous border or as a focal point plant.

Miscanthus sacchariflorus – waterfall shape.

Molinia caerulea subsp. arundinacea 'Karl Foerster' (Grass)

Soil: Moist, well drained, neutral to acid soil.
Aspect: Full sun/partial shade.
Growth habit: H up to 1.5m, W narrow at the base, wider at the top.
Season of interest: Year-round.
Design use: A tall, elegant grass of straight stems with arching green leaves. Looks good in a gravel garden, herbaceous border or as a focal point plant. It develops delicate panicles of seed heads which have a dark pink tinge to them.

ABOVE: *Molinia caerulea* subsp. *arundinacea* 'Karl Foerster'.

BELOW: *Rudbeckia fulgida*.

MIDDLE HEIGHT AND SMALL TRAPEZIUM/FAN SHAPED PLANTS

Rudbeckia fulgida (Herbaceous perennial)

Soil: Heavy but well drained soil that stays moist.
Aspect: Full sun/partial shade.
Growth habit: Up to H 1m × W 45cm.
Season of interest: Summer into autumn.
Design use: Sunny yellow flowers with dark centre, held on upright stems. Has a long flowering period. Gravel/prairie garden, herbaceous border.

Miscanthus sinensis 'Morning Light' (Grass)

Soil: Will tolerate most soils but best in a moist, well drained soil. Does not like excessive winter wet.
Aspect: Full sun/light shade.
Growth habit: H up to 1.2–1.5m, W narrow at the base, up to 60cm, wider at the top.
Season of interest: Year-round.
Design use: A medium sized, graceful grass which adds movement to a border; developing fluffy, cream coloured seed heads in the autumn which the birds love. Good as part of a gravel garden or herbaceous border. Seed heads continue to provide interest through the winter months.

Helenium 'Moerheim Beauty' (Herbaceous perennial)

Soil: Moist but well drained soil.
Aspect: Full sun.
Growth habit: Up to H 60cm × W 40cm.
Season of interest: Summer into autumn.
Design use: Excellent plant for a gravel/prairie garden, herbaceous border. With its deep terra-cotta flowers, with orange turning to brown cone-shaped centre, this plant will attract comment – it's a winner!

Season of interest: Spring, with green 'shuttle-cocks', then mid to late summer, when dark brown fronds are produced; these last through the winter when the green foliage has died down.
Design use: The distinct shuttlecock shape has strong visual impact. Woodland garden, damp border, waterside planting.

Carex testacea (Grass)

Soil: Moist, well drained.
Aspect: Full sun/partial shade.
Growth habit: H 20–30cm × W 20cm.
Season of interest: Year-round, evergreen grass.
Design use: Great little grass for permanent structure and colour at the front of a herbaceous border. Wonderful planted in groups or drifts.

Miscanthus sinensis 'Morning Light'.

Matteucia struthiopteris (Shuttlecock fern)

Soil: Moist, humus rich, well drained, neutral to slightly acid soil.
Aspect: Shade.
Growth habit: Up to H 40cm × W 20cm. It spreads by rhizomes and therefore produces other plants around itself.

ABOVE: *Matteuccia struthiopteris (fern)*.

LEFT: The dark terracotta of *Helenium* 'Moerheim Beauty'.

Has a lovely fresh green colour with bronze tinge. Good in a gravel garden. Its colour makes a striking contrast with a variety of colours.

Carex testacea.

Stipa tenuissima (Grass)

Soil: Moist, well drained.
Aspect: Full sun/partial shade.
Growth habit: H 30–40cm. W 20–30cm.
Season of interest: Year-round, evergreen grass.
Design use: Again, lovely grass for permanent structure at the front of a herbaceous border. Fantastic planted in groups or drifts. The wispy, pale coloured seed heads provide soft movement in the breeze. Good in a gravel garden or herbaceous border.

Stipa tenuissima.

OBLONG/RECTANGLE

Role and effect

This shape is man-made, usually achieved by clipping, and is commonly seen in the form of evergreen or deciduous hedging. Nonetheless, consider the structure that hedging brings to our landscape – dividing fields from each other and fields from roads, and creating a boundary between neighbouring gardens – it may be a simple shape but its effect is certainly not.

Historically, hedges were planted in the landscape to protect and demarcate the land for the owner, and to prevent cattle from straying into another herd.

Oblong/rectangle.

If the garden is large, hedges may be used to create division, separating the area into a series of 'rooms' or smaller spaces which are not only more easily managed, but provide the effect of a sense of journey and adventure through the garden, as one wonders what is beyond the hedge.

As previously mentioned, hedges are used to create a living boundary, in preference to a fence or wall, providing attractive screening and a wildlife habitat.

Groups of herbaceous plants, planted as drifts, naturally spread and grow as an oblong/rectangular group.

HEDGING, CLIPPED AND UNCLIPPED (ALL HARDY)

Carpinus betulus (Common hornbeam, clipped and unclipped)

Soil: Moderately fertile, well drained.
Aspect: Sun/partial shade.
Growth habit: H 1m after three years, W clip to 1m.
Season of interest: Year-round, even though deciduous.
Design use: Makes a strong, clipped hedging plant, which is dense and therefore good for a wind-break. Retains its autumn leaves until spring. It cannot be used for a narrow hedge because the base needs to be a minimum of 1m wide. Can produce catkins in spring. Plant 45cm apart and clip annually in late summer.

Fagus sylvatica (Common beech, clipped)

Soil: Tolerant of a wide range of soils including chalk, but not wet clay.
Aspect: Full sun/partial shade.
Growth habit: H 1.2m after six years, 1.5–2.5m after ten years × W 1m.
Season of interest: Year-round, retains its leaves through winter.
Design use: Makes a formal-looking clipped hedge that provides stunning autumn foliage colour. Plant 45cm apart, prune out the upper quarter of the shoots after planting and trim annually in summer. Beech is very slow to establish.

Ligustrum ovalifolium (Privet, clipped)

Soil: Well drained soil.
Aspect: Full sun/partial shade.
Growth habit: H 1m after two years × W 60–80cm, depending on whether single or double row planted.
Season of interest: Year-round. Hardy and evergreen.
Design use: Popular, fast-growing hedging plant. White flowers in spring. Also *Ligustrum ovalifolium* 'Aureum' available, which has a golden foliage colour.

Lonicera nitida (Chinese honeysuckle, clipped)

Soil: Well drained.
Aspect: Full sun/partial shade.
Growth habit: H 1m after three years. If allowed to grow over 1.2m, the hedge can split in the middle. Growing it with a chain link in the centre will help to prevent this. W Single row will make approx. 40–60cm.
Season of interest: Year-round. Hardy and evergreen.
Design use: Forms a dense small-leaved hedge.

Clipped
Carpinus
forming a
backdrop.

Unclipped *Carpinus betulus* (hornbeam) hedging.

Plant at 25–30cm spacings. Good for dwarf hedging.

Buxus sempervirens (Box, clipped)

Soil: Fertile, well drained.
Aspect: Prefers partial shade. Will tolerate full sun, but the combination of full sun and dry soil may encourage poor growth and dull foliage. Also renders the plant vulnerable to Buxus Blight.
Growth habit: H 60cm × W 30–40cm.
Season of interest: Year-round, hardy and evergreen.
Design use: Good for dwarf hedging to create a permanent edging to beds, either around flower or vegetable beds. Commonly used for knot gardens.

Lavandula spica and Lavandula angustifolia

Soil: Moderately fertile, well drained.
Aspect: Full sun.
Growth habit: H up to 80cm × W 80cm–1m.

Season of interest: Year-round, hardy and evergreen.
Design use: Makes an especially interesting permanent edging with its highly aromatic evergreen/grey foliage and intense mauve/blue flowers from early to late summer. Clip after flowering and you may get a second flush of flower. Excellent as any plant edging for softening path edges. Not long lived.

NATURALLY OCCURRING OBLONGS/RECTANGLES

Cornus controversa 'Variegata' (Naturally occurring shape)

Soil: Humus-rich, well drained soil. Neutral to acid.
Aspect: Sun/partial shade.
Growth habit: Up to H 15m × W 15m.
Season of interest: Year-round. Deciduous.
Design use: As a specimen tree, focal point plant. Variegated foliage provides spring into autumn interest and horizontal growth habit provides winter interest.

Clipped *Lonicera nitida*.

ABOVE: **Clipped *Buxus* forming dwarf rectangular hedging.**

BELOW: ***Buxus sempervirens:* dwarf hedging and topiary.**

ABOVE: **Lavender forming an elongated oblong edge.**

BELOW: **The natural 'rectangular' tiered growth habit of *Cornus controversa* 'Variegata'.**

Viburnum plicatum 'Lanarth' (Naturally occurring shape)

Soil: Moist but well drained.
Aspect: Full sun/partial shade.
Growth habit: Up to H 3m × W 4m in ten to twelve years.
Season of interest: Year-round.
Design use: As a specimen shrub, focal point plant. Fresh green foliage provides spring interest, bracts of white flowers provide late spring interest, deep purple foliage provides autumn interest and horizontal growth habit provides winter interest.

Achillea filipendulina 'Gold Plate' (Yarrow, herbaceous perennial)

Soil: Moist, well drained.
Aspect: Full sun.
Growth habit: Up to H 1.2m × W 45–50cm.

Season of interest: Summer, autumn and winter.
Design use: Floating rectangles of colour. Excellent long-flowering, tall, herbaceous plant for the border or gravel garden. Provides flattened

The horizontal growth habit of *Viburnum plicatum* 'Lanarth'.

Achillea filipendulina 'Gold Plate' – each individual flower head has an elongated oblong shape.

corymbs of deep, golden yellow flower heads, which turn to rich brown in autumn, providing architectural interest and a food source for the birds. Many other colours and heights available in this genus.

Echinacea purpurea (Coneflower, herbaceous perennial)

Soil: Humus rich, well drained.
Aspect: Full sun.
Growth habit: H up to 120– 150cm. W 45–60cm.
Season of interest: Summer, autumn and winter.
Design use: Floating rectangles of colour. Excellent long flowering, tall, herbaceous plant for the

Echinacea purpurea 'Magnus'.

border or gravel garden. Provides daisy-like flower heads with a central golden brown cone, surrounded by deep pink florets. Cones turn to rich brown in autumn, providing architectural interest and a food source for the birds. Many other colours and heights available in this genus.

RANDOM/IRREGULAR/ SPRAWLING/SPREADING

Role and effect

These plants have an interesting and very unusual growth habit: flattened, close to the ground and broad. Some indeed are described as ground hugging. Some of the larger species have more height, but all are far broader in width than they are in height.

This growth habit has the effect of widening the space – taking the eye outward across their width rather than upwards in height. This is still the case if the plants are closer to the ground, as in ground cover planting; the effect is simply at ground level. Ground cover plants tend to have a random shape, the effect of which is to bring a sense of informality to the area.

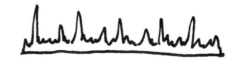

Random/spreading.

Ajuga reptans 'Black scallop' (Perennial)

Soil: Moist.
Aspect: Partial shade, some sun but not mid-day sun.
Growth habit: H 20cm × W infinite.
Season of interest: Evergreen. Year-round.
Design use: Excellent spring/early summer flowering ground cover plant. Several different foliage colours to choose from – all bear pale blue flower spikes from late spring through early summer.

Appearing to float: rectangles of colour.

Good value for money plant as it spreads by producing several plantlets on long shoots and therefore will cover a lot of ground. Good tough plant.

Geranium 'Ann Folkard' (Herbaceous perennial)

Soil: Well drained – some perennial geraniums will tolerate heavier soil, but not wet in the winter.
Aspect: Full sun/partial shade.
Growth habit: H 20–30cm × W up to 1.2m or more.
Season of interest: Early summer through to autumn.
Design use: Excellent ground cover perennial

with striking, dark centred, magenta pink flowers. Great in a gravel garden or border to create long periods of colour at ground level. Lovely orange/red foliage colour in autumn. Good, low maintenance plant which will romp away.

Veronica prostrata 'Loddon Blue' (Perennial)

Soil: Poor – moderately fertile soil. Well drained.
Aspect: Full sun.
Growth habit: Up to H 20cm × W 1m.
Season of interest: Year-round evergreen.
Design use: Excellent ground cover plant that is equally happy tumbling over a wall or raised bed, to soften the edge. In spring and summer produces small sky-blue flowers. Very small, glossy green leaves. Several varieties available, 'Oxford Blue' being one of the best.

Geranium 'Ann Folkard'.

Veronica prostrata 'Loddon Blue'.

Phlox subulata 'G.F. Wilson' (Perennial)

Soil: Well drained, fertile.
Aspect: Full sun.
Growth habit: H 10cm × W 30–40cm.
Season of interest: Evergreen, year-round.
Design use: Useful little ground cover plant for the alpine garden or raised bed. Provides year-round mat of greenery that for a few short weeks in spring produces a flush of soft lilac-blue flowers. Looks lovely cascading down a wall or raised bed. Worth having for its spring colour.

Phlox subulata 'G.F. Wilson'.

Gypsophila repens (Perennial)

Soil: Good soil that is slightly alkaline. Sharp drainage required.
Aspect: Full sun.
Growth habit: H 20–30cm × W 30–50cm.
Season of interest: Year-round.
Design use: A pretty, semi-evergreen plant that

Gypsophila repens.

produces delicate green/grey foliage. Through summer it produces a 'froth' of tiny pink flowers. Adds a sense of delicacy to any planting scheme.

Lamium maculatum 'Pink Nancy' (Perennial)

Soil: Moist, well drained.
Aspect: Deep/partial shade. This variety is variegated so partial shade is better.
Growth habit: H 20–25cm × W up to 1m.
Season of interest: Evergreen, year-round.
Design use: An excellent evergreen ground cover plant, which produces soft pink flowers in early summer. The flowers make a delicate contrast against the silver-green variegated foliage. Tough plant which brings 'light' spots to shady areas.

Ericas or heathers

Soil: Humus-rich, sharp, well drained, acidic soil.
Aspect: Full sun.
Growth habit: Up to H 20–30cm (depending upon variety.
Season of interest: Evergreen, year-round; autumn and spring flowering.
Design use: Plant in drifts. Colours available include whites, pale and dark pinks, and pale and dark mauves.

Thyme (Herb)

Soil: Well drained, low acidity – neutral.
Aspect: Full sun.
Growth habit: H 10cm × W 20–30cm.
Season of interest: Evergreen. Year-round.
Design use: Good for ground hugging evergreen areas in a herb or vegetable garden, front of a small bed or will tumble over edge of a raised bed. Aromatic foliage that can be green or variegated, producing sprays of tiny white or pink flowers in summer.

Geranium macrorrhizum (Perennial)

Soil: Will tolerate most soils, but not waterlogged in winter.

The random, spreading habit of ericas.

Aspect: Full sun/partial shade.
Growth habit: H 20cm × W 1.2–1.5m; wide spreading and could be more as spreads by rhizomes producing new plants.
Season of interest: Semi-evergreen, year-round.
Design use: Excellent, tough, semi-evergreen ground cover plant. It has aromatic foliage that produces flowers ranging in colour from the soft pink *Geranium macrorrhizum* 'Ingerswen's Variety' to the white *Geranium macrorrhizum* 'Album' and the loud crimson/purple flowers of *Geranium macrorrhizum* 'Bevan's Variety'. Rhizomes can be broken off and planted to increase areas of planting. Good for gravel garden, front of herbaceous border, rockeries, and areas of partial shade. The soft green foliage turns to orange/red in autumn, providing interest through the winter.

Geranium macrorrhizum.

Bergenia (Perennial)

Soil: Will tolerate many soils.
Aspect: Full sun/partial shade.
Growth habit: H 20–30cm × W 1.2–1.5m; wide spreading and could be more as spreads by rhizomes producing new plants.
Season of interest: Evergreen. Year-round.
Design use: Tough, evergreen plant with large leaves. Many different varieties available – some

Thymus genus.

Bergenia – evergreen ground cover.

with green and some with dark red foliage. Flowers in early spring and again there is a wide choice of flower colour from white to pale pink to bright magenta pink. All will tolerate dry conditions and will cover large areas of ground with their large glossy leaves like 'elephant's ears'. Good for gravel garden, narrow border at base of a wall, front of border.

PROSTRATE

The prostrate growth habit of evergreen conifers is very regular, producing a strongly defined, broad shape and bringing a sense of formality. Some varieties provide this at a lower level, up to approximately 45cm, whilst others grow taller, up to approximately 1m.

Role and effect

Such is the strength of their shape, the mature prostrate conifer will act as a focal point plant, providing permanent structure and strong architectural interest, almost like a living sculpture.

Prostrate.

This plant family has amongst its members some lovely foliage colours, from fresh greens to striking blues and yellows, which when coupled with the fascinating shapes makes for not just a plant shape of strong visual impact, but a 'colourful' shape as well.

SOME PROSTRATE GROWING CONIFER VARIETIES

Juniperus communis 'Green Carpet' (Conifer)

Soil: Any well drained soil, will tolerate chalky, dry and sandy soils.
Aspect: Full sun/light dappled shade.
Growth habit: H 50–60cm × W 1–6m in ten to fifteen years.
Season of interest: Evergreen. Year-round.
Design use: Can be used as focal point plant once it becomes more mature. Makes dense ground cover. Good plant association with heathers, azaleas and rhododendrons. Will provide architectural interest through the winter months.

Juniperus communis 'Depressa Aurea' – conifer

Soil: Any well drained soil, will tolerate chalky, dry and sandy soils.

Juniperus communis 'Green Carpet'.

Aspect: Full sun/light dappled shade.

Growth habit: H 60cm × W 1.5m.

Season of interest: Evergreen. Year-round.

Design use: Has golden yellow colour which makes for a strong contrast and splash of sunshine wherever it is used. Can be used as focal point plant once it becomes more mature. Will provide architectural interest through the winter months.

Juniperus x *media* (Conifer)

Soil: Any well drained soil, will tolerate chalky, dry and sandy soils.

Aspect: Full sun/light dappled shade.

Growth habit: Up to H 1.2m × W 2–3m in ten to fifteen years.

Season of interest: Evergreen. Year-round.

Design use: Can be used as focal point plant once it becomes more mature. Makes dense ground cover. Good plant association with heathers, azaleas and rhododendrons. Will provide architectural interest through the winter months.

Juniperus squamata 'Hunnetorp' (Conifer)

Soil: Any well drained soil, will tolerate chalky, dry and sandy soils.

Aspect: Full sun/light dappled shade.

Growth habit: H 50–60cm. W 1.5–2m.

Season of interest: Evergreen. Year-round.

Design use: Can be used as a focal point plant once it becomes more mature. Makes dense, evergreen, ground cover and associates well with heathers, azaleas and rhododendrons. Provides architectural interest through the winter months.

In this chapter we have defined each plant as a visual graphic that can be easily reproduced. You also have an informative plant list and a photo gallery of as many plant shapes as possible; in time, when thinking of a plant shape, the plant names will automatically spring to mind. You therefore have a good foundation for the next step, learning about the plant shapes method. Chapters 5 and 6 together provide everything you need to produce your first '3D' planting design sketch.

Juniperus x *media*.

Juniperus squamata 'Hunnetorp'.

Trees provide an irregular 'outline' shape when in leaf, which transforms into a 'skeletal' shape through the winter months.

6 THE PLANT SHAPES METHOD

The plant shapes method is a logical progression of eight steps, culminating in a planting design sketch which has depth. When first using the method it is best to practise on small planting areas that can be increased in size as confidence with the method grows.

The following sketches and notes demonstrate the method and are based on a border 10m long by approximately 3m in depth. Of course, in reality there are many, many variations in border shape and size; however, once you have understood the process you can apply it to any of these variations. When you are confident, you will be able to stand in front of a border and make a freehand sketch of its outline shape, estimate its size, add some plant shapes and then develop this to the final planting scheme stage. If the border is large, it can be divided into smaller sections – counting fence panels is useful for this and for estimating the size.

The 'overlay method' at the end of the chapter is an additional technique that can be used in conjunction with the plant shapes method.

THE PROCESS

It is important when developing a planting scheme to have a 'plan'; after all, you would not set out on a complicated journey without a map! The 'plan' consists of two parts:

- Writing the 'wish list' or 'requirements' of the scheme.
- Listing the technical considerations and choices that need to be made.

We shall then use the plan to work through the remaining steps of the plant shapes method. You may be making the plan for your own garden, in which case you know what you require but will find it useful to organize the information. Or your planting scheme may be determined by a client, in response to a series of questions you have asked regarding their very personal ideas, likes and dislikes about how they wish the planting area to look. You can pick and choose from the 'wish list' below.

Step 1: the 'wish list'

It is useful to think of your wish list in terms of plant groups, which provides a structure for the work. You need to bear in mind the following factors.

Seasonal interest

- **Trees** Evergreens (usually conifers)? Large or small (depends on size of garden and/or border)? Deciduous, large or small (depends on size of garden and/or border)? Spring or

DRAWING EQUIPMENT NEEDED

Scale ruler 1:50 or 1:100.
HB or 2H pencil – a harder pencil is preferable as there is less smudging.
A rubber.
A pad of A4 or A3 drawing paper.
A good plant book such as the *RHS A–Z Encyclopaedia of Garden Plants* – an excellent plant reference book that provides lots of images and plant information such as soil requirement, height and width, flowering season, and much more.

summer flowering? Autumn foliage colour? Berries?

- **Shrubs** Evergreen or deciduous? Spring or summer flowering? Autumn foliage colour? Berries? Scent?
- **Herbaceous** Spring, summer or autumn? Flower, grasses or ferns?
- **Bulbs** Late winter/early spring, summer, autumn?
- **Climbers** Early spring, summer or winter? Evergreen or deciduous? Flower? Scent?

Colour

What colours do I want? How can I obtain them? (There is more about how to choose colours in Chapter 7.)

- **Flower colour** Which season? Shrub, herbaceous, climber or bulb? What colour or colours?
- **Foliage colour** Which season? Tree, shrub or climber? What colour: yellow, red, orange, russet?
- **Herbaceous perennials** die down in the autumn so they will only provide the chosen colour during the summer months, though there are some that provide late spring and autumn flower colour. Some herbaceous perennials retain very interesting, architectural seed heads – the *Eryngium* and *Helenium* genera, to name just two.
- **Deciduous trees and shrubs** will drop their leaves in autumn and will therefore provide a

skeletal shape through winter; this can look fantastic covered in snow or frost in the winter. Some trees and shrubs produce berries that will hold until late winter, when most will have been eaten by the birds. Some shrubs produce flowers on bare stems in very early spring – some of the best scented varieties are *Lonicera fragrantissima*, *Chimonanthus praecox* and the *Chaenomeles* genus. The *Cornus* genus provides a wide range of striking stem colour throughout the winter, once their leaves have dropped.

- **Grasses** Few are evergreen, most are deciduous, dying back to a creamy beige, straw-like colour. Their winter interest is in the seed heads: some are fluffy, others have more tiny, bead-like seed heads, but all provide striking architectural shape and movement, through the winter, as well as being a food source for wildlife.

Step 2: the outline

Draw a rough outline of the area to be planted. Use 2m-high fencing as a visual aid to scale (standard fencing panels come in a variety of sizes, the tallest being 2m).

Step 3: structural shapes and technical considerations

Decide where the main structural shapes (permanent structure) are to be. The second part of your

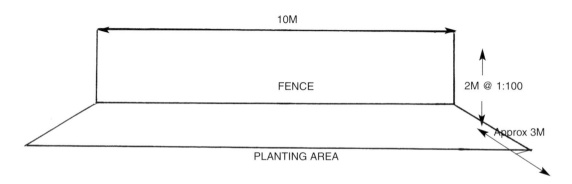

Using fence height as a visual aid to scale.

plan is 'Listing the technical considerations and choices that need to be made'. These should be given due time and attention in order to achieve the best possible planting scheme for the area concerned.

Considerations

The following considerations refer to the initial plant choices made, which will form the main structure for the scheme.

- Whichever shape I choose, what role is it going to play? (Review 'Role and effect' for shape chosen, see Chapter 5.)
- Do I require a permanent effect? If so, evergreens should be chosen.
- Do I require the 'effect' to change? For example, a deciduous, spring-flowering shrub will be in flower in spring, followed by leaf through spring, summer and into autumn, when it drops its leaves; the 'effect' provided then changes again to an outline skeletal

shape that often looks incredible when covered in frost. So several effects are provided by one plant – a sequence of effects occurring through several seasons.

- Is one plant of this shape sufficient? What is the effect with repetition of this shape?
- What is the effect of combining permanent structure plant shapes?
- Are the shapes in balance?

Your permanent structure could be, for example, a central focal point, evergreen with a strong shape such as a conifer, or maybe a shorter standard bay tree (globe with height) at each end of the border. There are many choices available, but broadly speaking if thought of as evergreen or deciduous, by experimenting with the plant shapes you can decide which the best option is.

Once the permanent structural shapes have been decided and sketched in, add written notes alongside as an aide-memoire as to whether they

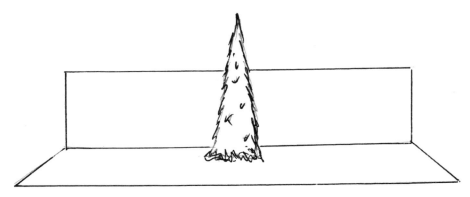

Central cone as the main structural shape.

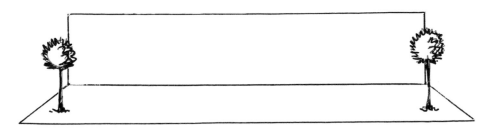

Globe of clipped box; the shape is taller with the stem.

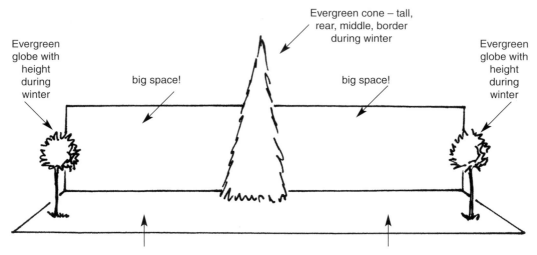

Choosing permanent structure plants and making notes as an aide-memoire.

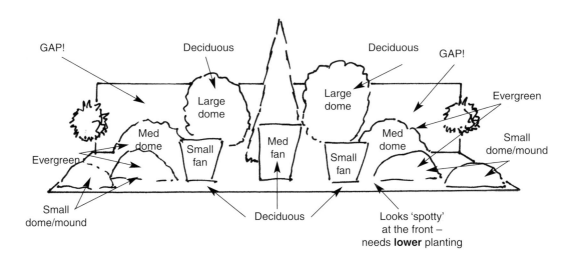

Adding more shapes and notation, assessing the scheme as it develops.

are deciduous or evergreen, and the effect as you see it.

Step 4: developing the planting scheme

Gradually develop the planting scheme, adding more shapes and notation. The notation at this stage refers to the chosen shape – whether it is evergreen or deciduous, plus any thoughts you have about the scheme.

The aim at this stage is to achieve a scheme that has balance in its use of shapes, through a balanced selection of evergreen and deciduous trees and shrubs, and the addition of some colourful herbaceous perennials, architectural grasses, and short-lived but welcome colour from bulbs – all providing interest throughout the seasons. The trick is to select plants from each plant group.

Step 5: add more shapes

Taking note of your observations, continue to add more shapes until you are satisfied that the scheme is balanced in terms of shapes and shape combinations, plant heights and widths.

Step 6: further development

Note the plant group, colour and season required. Even if you are not confident with plant groups, have a go – it can be amended later. Also note colour and the season in which the colour is required.

Step 7: add colour

Even though optional, I cannot emphasize strongly enough the importance of taking time to explore the effects of the plant qualities so far chosen. You should be getting a clearer picture in your minds' eye of the structure of the scheme; now the real fun begins with adding colour. The addition of colour greatly increases the visual qualities of the planting scheme, making it far more realistic and giving a more defined picture of what we will see. We would not plant a black and white scheme!

For further exploration with colour, try adding colour for a particular season and see the variation that the different seasons bring. This can be done by using tracing paper over the sketched scheme.

Step 8: name the plants

This is the point at which the plant shapes method really comes into its own and the work done so far becomes the basis for plant research, in order to choose and name plants. The drawings with notes are full of information that will speed up the time spent in choosing and naming plants. This is because when the traditional method of working up a planting scheme is used, the plant list is drafted first. This depends upon an already existing base of plant knowledge, which can take many years of study, reading plant books and experience to acquire. By using the plant shapes method, you have already decided the plant group, shape and size you want, the flowering season, flower, foliage or berries interest, and so on. So at this point of naming the plants, you have all of this information on which to base the research and formulate your plant list. Rather than racking your brains in an attempt to recall those plant names that you *do* know, or spending copious hours trawling through books not knowing what you are looking for, you can

- take paper and pen and organize the noted information;

Adding more shapes and filling the gaps.

Evergreen
all year

Evergreen,
late spring, white

Evergreen
all year

Deciduous – pink,
spring

Evergreen
all year

Evergreen
all year

Evergreen
all year

Evergreen
all year

Bamboo

Shrub

Shrub

Climber

Evergreen

Decid
Grass

Evergreen
Shrub

Decid

Decid

Decid

Decid

Decid

Evergreen
all year

Autumn
foliage
colour

Berries

Orange
herbaceous

Evergreen
all year

Orange
herbaceous

Pale yellow
summer

White summer
sub shrub

Permanent ground-
cover herbaceous

Adding the plant group, colour and season required.

Adding colour brings the scheme to life.
In all its glory – summer.

Exploring how it looks in a different
season – early winter.

TREES		CONIFERS – YEAR ROUND	
Season & Interest	**Name**	**Season & Interest**	**Name**
Spring flower		Green, tall cone shape	*Thuja* 'Smaragd'
Autumn berries	*Sorbus aucuparia*		
		Small, rounded	*Picea* 'Nana'
Summer flower		Blue, prostrate	*Juniperus* 'Blue Star'
Leaf shape & autumn foliage colour	*Liquidambar styraciflua*		

SHRUBS		HERBACEOUS FLOWERS	
Season & Interest	**Name**	**Season & Interest**	**Name**
Spring flower – pink/white	*Viburnum* 'Eve Price'	Spring, blue, low	*Geranium* 'Johnsons Blue'
Autumn berries, spring foliage, autumn foliage	*Amelanchier* 'Lanarth'	Summer/autumn Pink, tall	*'Echinacea'* Magnus' Lupin Phlox
Late winter early spring flower scented	*Sarcococca confusa* – med *Lonicera fragrantissima* – lge	Summer/autumn Tall, yellow	Sunflower *Verbascum*
Summer foliage Colour – yellow	*Philadelphus* 'Aurea'	Autumn, orange	*Hemerocallis*
Autumn berries	*Pyracantha* / *Berberis*		

HERBACEOUS GRASSES & FERNS		BULBS & CLIMBERS	
Season & Interest	**Name**	**Season & Interest**	**Name**
Spring, flowerhead	*Stipa gigantea* – grass	Spring, yellow	*Narcissus*
Summer, evergreen, colour	*Carex testacea* – grass	Spring, mixed colours Summer, tall. Mixed colours Autumn – orange Evergreen Summer flower, scent	*Crocus* *Gladioli* *Crocosmia* *Hedera* *Jasminum officinale*

Organizing the information.

- list the noted plant qualities in a 'season and interest' column;
- as you research, note firstly the plant genus, and finally the *variety* in a 'name' column.

So far we have been working on a rough plan of the area. This does not mean that the scheme should not later be drawn to scale; in the case of the professional garden designer this is a must. For the professional, drawing a scaled planting plan serves the purpose of ensuring that the planting scheme 'fits' the area for five to ten years,

and enables the designer to quantify and cost the plants. Notes can also be made on the plan of any problem areas, soil preparation required and plant specification notes. There are other elements to a professional planting plan that can be seen in Chapter 8.

A further purpose of the plan is to serve as a visual aid when describing the proposed scheme to the client, particularly if a colour overlay has been prepared; the 'plant shape' sketches are an excellent three-dimensional visual aid.

The plant shapes method is equally useful and

valuable to the professional prior to drawing the scheme up to scale, and to the amateur who wants to explore various planting options and how they look, or a variety of colour schemes.

THE OVERLAY METHOD

The overlay method has been around in the world of garden design for many years. It is a technique that enables the designer to produce a visual image of what is being proposed, so that the client can clearly see the intended final result, and the user of the garden can very quickly explore several options. It is thus of enormous value to both the designer and client and the user. The technique entails drawing on tracing paper over a very accurate photograph that gives a sense of perspective. Perhaps even more importantly, it saves a lot of time – and time is money to the designer. It also reduces the number of expensive wrong plant choices, because the experimentation has taken place on paper prior to any money being spent on plants.

For the professional designer, I am not suggesting that this method should be used to replace the practice of producing visualization drawings using conventional techniques and skills, but it can be regarded as another tool with which to produce visuals.

- Take photographs of the planted area in its existing state. Try to take the pictures at the same level; if necessary they can then be cropped and joined using a software programme which is digital image friendly. This gives a more accurate representation of the area.
- Print out one, or several, hard copies of the image; A4 size should be satisfactory in landscape orientation.
- Place a piece of tracing paper (the greaseproof type that can be easily seen through) over the photograph and secure with tape.

Sketching shapes on trace overlay.

Before.

- Using pencil or black pen, draw in plant shapes in the areas where the border seems to be lacking something – these sketches are so quick to do that several can be done until the best arrangement is found.
- Now add handwritten notes as in the previous method, recording thoughts and plant characteristics.

As with the plant shapes method, this technique can be applied to small gardens in their entirety or, in the case of a larger garden, the area can be divided into smaller sections – this would be particularly appropriate when using digital images of each area.

The areas to be redesigned can also be measured up in order to draft a scaled planting plan. By recording photographs in a logical, easy to remember sequence such as 'left border, from 1m to 5m', 'from 5m to 10m' and so on, which tallies with the survey information, the photographs will act as an accurate record of the area to be redesigned.

You can see from this description that the overlay method is quick, accurate and avoids all the crises of confidence when it comes to drawing skills. In fact, I would suggest that it builds confidence in drafting hand sketches.

After.

7 USING COLOUR

What a dull world this would be if everything were seen in black and white; a few shades of grey might make it more interesting, but only marginally. Colour, in combination with several other elements, is a major contributor to planting interest. It is human nature to want to see colour; remember how energized and uplifted we feel in the summer months when we are surrounded by and immersed in colour; and conversely, how dull our surroundings can look in the grey of winter.

To provide colour in the garden, the season in which the colour is required will influence the plant group chosen. Plant selection will generally be from several groups to provide a succession of colour and interest. It is not until we delve more deeply into the world of plants, textiles or wall paints that we become aware of the whole range of shades within, for example, 'pink' or 'blue', that are available to us, and this is most certainly the case when choosing plants.

The strongest triggers for human memory are scent and vision; in the plant world these often go hand in hand, but colour stimulates our visual attention with the secondary effect of a *reaction*. In a garden, colour is the most striking element that engages us almost immediately. How does it do this? And how, when designing a planting scheme, can we use this to our advantage?

It is vital that we have an understanding of the use of colour and its resultant effects. On the one hand we aim to create a successful planting scheme that the onlooker finds visually attractive and emotionally comfortable; looking at the garden is an enjoyable experience. On the other hand, the long-term aim is to create this experience throughout the seasons, so our knowledge and the resultant plant choices need to address and fulfil both of these criteria.

THE USE AND EFFECTS OF COLOUR

Colour theory

Entire books have been written on the subject of colour, so here colour theory has been condensed to provide enough background information to inform the plant choices to be made. This chapter focuses on the use of colour in relation to plants. Interestingly, without their colour, plants would not survive or even grow in the first place. Nature in its cleverness provides that flowers have colour in order to attract insects, particularly bees, for pollination, which ensures the setting of seed and subsequent plants being produced so that the survival of the plant is ensured. Bees can see yellow, orange, yellow/green, blue/green, blue, purple and violet, so by including plants of these colours in a garden, we can assist nature by supporting bees – and also have beautiful gardens.

Colour and light
When light is reflected off the surface of an object, we perceive colour; in the context of a garden, flowers and leaves are 'the object'. Green is the predominant garden colour; grass, for example, contains a pigment called chlorophyll that absorbs the wavelengths of all colours in the visible spectrum except one. This one is reflected away from the grass and we see it as green; the same applies in varying degrees to leaves – hence

OPPOSITE: **Colour contrast of Rudbeckia and Asters.** (Photo: Rhoda Nottridge)

the wide variety of green, yellow/green and blue/green foliage colours available.

Colour intensity depends upon the light absorption properties of the surface of an object. For example, a black surface absorbs all colours and nothing is reflected back, so we see black. Conversely, a white surface reflects all wavelengths and the combination of all colours in light results in white. The parallel of this with respect to plants is a leaf with a matt surface or a glossy surface: the matt surface absorbing light and the glossy surface reflecting light.

Plant colours are created by pigments; these are substances in the leaf or petal that absorb colour. Bright colours such as yellow, orange and red are caused by 'carotenoids'; 'quinones' cause yellow, orange, red, purple or green; and 'flavenoids' cause yellow and bluish reds.

Colour use

Generally speaking, when creating a planting scheme we seek to 'please the eye'. What would be the point of creating a scheme that was not pleasant to look at? Even Christopher Lloyd, who challenged traditional colour use by planting bold, strong, some might say 'clashes' of colour together, was selective in his choice of, for example, which magenta pink gave a pleasing effect when planted with a carefully selected yellow. In spite of his choices looking random, they certainly were not.

Colour use in planting can be broadly divided into two categories: creating schemes using *harmony* and *contrast*.

Harmony

To create a planting scheme that is pleasant to look at, we must consider some principles of colour harmony. Colours are harmonious when a dominant colour and tone run through the entire scheme, unifying and pulling it together. For instance, blue delphiniums are commonly seen in summer flowering borders; the blue can be picked up in other plants, such as intense blue *Salvia* and the soft blue of *Nepeta*. The blue, repeated at regular intervals and in various shades/tones throughout the scheme, provides continuity and unites the scheme.

Contrast

Sometimes when looking at a planting scheme it seems dull and lacking in 'life'; all the plants seem to merge together to form a mass within which there is nothing particularly interesting. However, if a plant of contrasting colour is added, the whole thing comes to life; it becomes interesting to look at and exciting. But a word of caution: too much contrast will create disharmony, making the scheme seem brash and offensive to the eye. Some examples of successful colour contrasts are purple and red, orange and blue, blue and yellow.

The cool blue flowers and silver stems of *Nepeta* 'Six Hills Giant'.

The hot red of *Dahlia* 'Bishop of Llandaff'.

Moods and emotions

Colour is very emotive: we all react to it in some way, some people being more sensitive to colour than others. For instance, if we walk into a room, a particular colour may not be noticed, but there will be a definite sense of either feeling uplifted and energized, or depressed and flat; exactly the same experience is felt in a garden, and the experience of a garden will vary from person to person, depending on their sensitivity to colour and the colours in the garden.

Effects

Colour is profound in its effects: cool colours such as some blues, greys and cool greens, for example, can be used to create a sense of calm and tranquillity – ideal colour choices for a play area used by children who need a calming environment for outdoor activity, whether play, learning or time out. A cool colour scheme can also be used in a very hot, south facing area to create a

The cool lilac of iris and alliums.

relaxed atmosphere. Blues can also be 'warm' if they have red or lilac tones.

Conversely, hot colours such as reds, oranges, and some yellows (depending on their intensity) can be used to energize and stimulate an area. Their use is ideal for an area used by people who suffer from depression, or in a rundown area that needs uplifting.

Tricks with colour

Spatial effects

A long, narrow garden can be made to appear wider by placing hot colours, particularly red, on the far boundary. Red *foreshortens*, making the boundary appear closer than it is, and therefore the garden appears shorter.

A short, wide garden can be made to appear longer by placing cool colours, such as blues and whites, on the far boundary. Blue *recedes*, making the boundary appear further away, and therefore the garden appears longer.

To draw attention to a particular area in a garden or bed, use reds and oranges; the foreshortening effect makes them appear to 'jump out', therefore dominating and commanding visual attention.

The hot orange-red of *Helenium* 'Moerheim Beauty'.

To detract from an unpleasant view or area, plant blues to make the area appear to recede into the distance; or plant reds away from the unpleasant view to command visual attention.

If a garden area feels cool, probably because it receives less sun, introduce plants that have bright red/greens and yellow/greens to enliven and warm the area. Conversely, to cool a hot garden area down introduce grey and blue/green plants.

An area that appears dark and shady can be lifted and lightened by introducing whites, creams and pale yellows, mostly found in variegated foliage. The hosta family offers a vast variety of foliage colours, but being herbaceous will die down during the winter months. The euonymus family offers a good choice of variegated foliage which is evergreen, so providing the lighter effect permanently.

Shape

Our attention is also taken by the recognition of strong shapes, usually in the form of evergreen conifers. This is due to the fact that not only are they bold in shape, but they also have a strongly defined outline. The form is defined by the jewel-like deep emerald greens, the soft, cool, blue greys and the uplifting, sunny golden yellows available from this family. It is almost as if a second garden appears when everything else has died down for winter, as the form and foliage colour of the conifer shapes come into their own at this time of year – they are impossible to ignore. It is possible to create a garden of permanent interest, which provides colour and form, from the heather and conifer families alone; however, the soil needs to be acidic and moist for the plants to thrive.

The cool blue flowers and silver stems of *Perovskia*.

A mixed border demonstrating how red 'jumps out'.

Foliage colour

Most garden colour is provided by flowers, we think. But let us not forget the impact of foliage colour, and the stunning autumn colours that this season provides. Plant foliage colour offers the garden a second helping. Its use is twofold: there is the foliage colour of a plant throughout most of the season, followed by its autumn foliage colour that provides an extended season of interest.

This is an important aspect of planting design to bear in mind when choosing a plant, in order to provide 'value for money' that translates into a planting scheme that is not just of interest during the summer but performs throughout the four seasons. There are many shrubs, such as the ever-green *Pittosporum* genus, which include a selection of stunning foliage colour all year round and subtle changes in leaf colour in autumn. The acer family has many, many members that cannot fail to please when changing to their autumn colours. Westonbirt Arboretum has some fabulous exam-ples and is well worth a visit, just to see the array of autumn foliage colour provided by its collection of acers.

Autumn is a time when, by selecting plants for their quality of warm autumnal foliage colour, the season of interest is extended until temperatures drop and the leaves fall.

Winter interest: stems and berries

Autumn is not the end of it. Colour can be provided and the season of interest extended into winter by including in the planting scheme some plants, usually shrubs, that produce either coloured stems (the *Cornus* family) or brightly coloured berries. The latter include *Callicarpa bodinieri* var. *giraldii* 'Profusion', with its unusual lilac berries looking like clusters of beads; or *Viburnum opulus* with its bunches of glossy, bright red berries; and, old-fashioned maybe, *Cotoneaster horizontalis*, which produces so many scarlet berries that the stem can hardly be seen.

Warm autumn foliage colour.

welcome added bonus of including berry-producing shrubs in a planting scheme is that they provide a winter food source for wildlife, particularly birds. So not only do we have the pleasure of looking at the berries, but also of watching birds feed on them during the winter months.

Winter interest can also be satisfied by selecting plants, usually shrubs, for their coloured stems, which take the leading role once the leaves have dropped. The finest of this plant group, the *Cornus* family, offers us deep pink, red, bright lime green, deep chocolate brown, and orange stems. When repeat planted they provide almost all the interest required for the winter months.

In summary, colour use in planting is a skill that is best learnt through experience – though this does not have to be at the expense of a client! Take a trip to a nursery or garden centre and look at how the plants are displayed, maybe pull some plants out and experiment (please put them back

Other shrubs that produce berries in profusion are the *Pyracantha* and *Berberis* families. A

ABOVE: **Bright red bead-like berries of *Viburnum opulus*.**

LEFT: ***Acer palmatum* 'Sango-kaku': leaf and stem autumn colour.**

in their correct place if you do this). Walk around your local neighbourhood and take photographs, as many as you can, of plantings that are of interest all through the year, particularly of gardens that look good in the winter. Get the images up on your computer and analyse what it is about them that is of interest.

There is one variable in every garden that can only be assessed in each individual garden, and that is the light. Light intensity, by its very nature, changes colour; this is where it is important to have assessed the light conditions in the given planting area prior to choosing plants. Knowing the aspect, whether it is north, south, east or west facing, will provide valuable information for this process.

Primarily, for the chosen colours to perform successfully in a planting scheme we need to consider the elements of colour theory that are relevant to plant selection: aspect, contrast, harmony and effects. Secondly, we need to consider colour from an organic perspective, that is, the colour provided by our chosen plant group and how and when the chosen plant is going to provide that colour. So, for example, we choose a shrub that is going to provide us with spring flower, summer and autumn foliage colour and berries through the winter. Or a herbaceous plant that is going to provide a burst of intense colour through the summer only. The key to a successful scheme is that throughout the changes that take place in each season, there is something to hold interest all through the year.

A hot border of oranges and yellows.

8 EXAMPLES OF PLANTING DESIGN SCHEMES

A scheme that relies on permanent form with additional interest of an underplanting of strong foliage shape and colour.

The successful establishment of a planting scheme is dependent upon the plants being provided with a suitable growing environment, an environment that is a combination of right aspect and optimum soil conditions. Having said that, if a plant is provided with a soil that is open in texture, nutritious and has available water, the aspect is a secondary requirement inasmuch as plants will survive in a less than ideal situation, but they will not thrive. The flowering habit, leaf colour and ultimate size of the plant will all be adversely affected. As a consequence, this chapter looks at soil facts and remedial treatments in conjunction with the planting examples.

When a planting scheme is in the development stage, it is advisable to explore a variety of planting options for the given site, in order that the best possible choices are made and the scheme performs throughout the year. The plant shapes sketch method is ideal for this, making the exploratory stage of the process quick and easy; it is a method that can be used by the professional on site or at the drawing board, or by the amateur in the garden or at the kitchen table.

When the final sketch of shapes has been decided, in order to select suitably sized plants and quantify plant numbers, the scheme will need to be drawn to scale. This can be done using the accepted planting plan format that you will be shown in this chapter. You will also see a selection of schemes, each for a specific growing environment; each scheme is shown as a plant shapes sketch and in planting plan format to a scale of 1:50.

THE PLANTING PLAN

Format

Planting plan format is a graphical method of presenting a planting scheme, in plan and drawn to scale, usually 1:50 or for larger sites 1:100. The scaled planting plan is a working document, usually produced by the professional garden designer, which is used to demonstrate the proposed scheme and colours to the client, to calculate plant numbers, and to enable the designer or contractor to set out the plants according to the plan. That is not to say that the amateur gardener cannot attempt to produce a scaled planting plan if they so wish.

The chosen plants are represented by circles, drawn with a compass or circle template. Most planting plans are drawn to represent the scheme in seven to ten years time; so, for example, a large shrub such as *Viburnum tinus* 'Eve Price' is going to reach approximately 2–3m in height and width within this time scale. However, a word of caution: plant growth rates will be affected by weather, aspect and soil conditions, thus altering the eventual size of the mature specimen; so this type of information is intended as a guideline only.

On the planting plan the *Viburnum* will be represented at 1:50 by a circle about 3cm in diameter. The circle is then labelled with the plant name and the number of specimens required (see the examples below of planting schemes for damp shade). When designing a planting scheme, it is usual to draw in the 'structural' plants as a first step, that is, large evergreen plants that form the bulk of the scheme.

Process

1. Check the planting brief for any special requests: for example, favourite colours or plants.
2. Compile the plant list, choosing structural plants first. Make your plant selection from up-to-date lists to ensure that selected plants are available.
3. Draw the planting areas to scale in pencil on tracing paper.
4. Draw in structural plants first, to scale; a variety of graphics can be used to distinguish plants.
5. As you are working, continually review what has been done and consider the balance of deciduous and evergreen and seasonal interest. Herbaceous plants can be drawn as multiple circles or a named drift, each plant represented by a 'x'; allow 30–40cm spacing between each plant, maybe 50cm if it is a herbaceous plant that is going to become large.
6. As you work, continually update the plant list quantity, as this is much easier to do as you go. Amend any changes in genus and/or variety.
7. Once the planting scheme is to your satisfaction, apply colour to a trace overlay and prepare any visualization sketches you wish to use.
8. On the PC, set up a file in the client or project name and transfer images of as many of the proposed plants as possible. If a PC is not available, a montage of pictures of the plants can be made.
9. Prepare the cost estimate, including any

materials such as topsoil for soil preparation and/or tree bark mulch if required, plus labour and delivery charges.

10. Organize a planting sketch design meeting with the client.

11. At this meeting, any changes to the proposed scheme can be made very easily, as it is all in pencil. Remember to adjust estimate accordingly.

12. Aim to have agreed any changes by the conclusion of the meeting; you may need to contact the client post meeting with a re-cost. Once the cost has been accepted, the final draft planting plan can be prepared – inked up, together with the plant schedule, and printed.

13. Apply colour render to client copy, and provide black and white copies for contractors.

PLANTING EXAMPLES

Damp shade

This difficult growing environment is commonly found in the north and north-east facing aspect of a garden, particularly if the soil is of clay content. Shade can also be created by tall structures such as fencing, sheds and garages, housing on the boundary, or tall, dense hedging, in which case it may become dry in the summer.

In the case of heavy clay, which is cloddy and cracks in the summer months due to drying out, considerable soil preparation should be carried out to provide a suitable growing medium for plants.

Soil preparation

All plants, when newly planted, need to establish a root system in order to draw water and nutrients from the soil, and for stabilization; therefore, to allow the plant to do this, the soil structure needs to be of an open, aerated, moist but not wet nature.

The addition of sharp grit and well-rotted compost, or soil conditioner, in order to break the soil up and aerate it (about a bucket of each per square metre) will provide the plants with a soil which roots can penetrate. It may be necessary, if the soil is particularly wet and heavy, to also add topsoil. It is not advisable to add manure, as this is a wet material and can increase the 'stickiness' rather than improve it.

The application of a layer of tree bark on the soil surface, to a depth of approximately 75–100mm, will also help to break the soil down as the tree bark decomposes. By covering the soil surface, the tree bark mulch will also reduce evaporation during the summer months, assisting in the prevention of cracking and drying out to an impenetrable, iron hard surface. The tree bark will need topping up every two to three years, and the smaller the grade of chip the better: tree bark that contains large curly chunks provides a breeding site and hiding place for slugs, and that particular garden visitor is not a welcome one.

Dry, sunny

This is a far more favourable growing environment, commonly found in the south and south-west aspect of a garden. These are preferable conditions for the establishment of plants, as the loose soil structure allows the plant roots to penetrate easily, particularly if the soil is both moist and free draining in nature. However, free draining soil can carry its own problems, in that it dries out very quickly during hot summer months, so new plantings will need frequent watering until established. Dry, free draining soil can be a 'hungry' soil, due to the washing out of nutrients as water drains through; therefore it also needs soil improvement and regular feeding.

Soil preparation

To improve both the structure and water retention properties of a dry, sandy, free draining soil, regular applications of manure, well-rotted compost and leaf mould are all well-known treatments. A 'loamy' free draining soil will not have these problems and is, in fact, almost the perfect soil.

The application of tree bark mulch will, in this

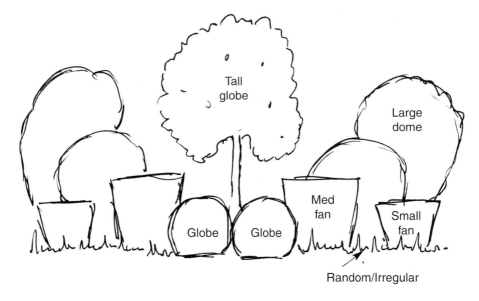

Planting scheme for damp shade with some clay, drawn with plant shapes.

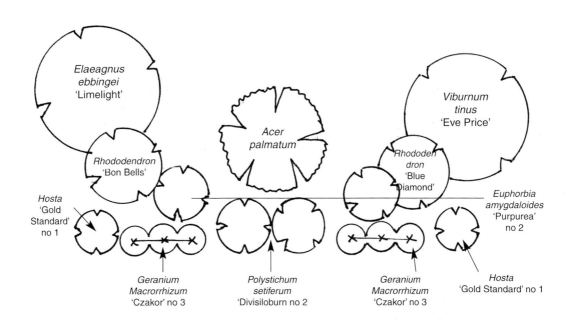

Planting scheme for damp shade with some clay, drawn as a planting plan, to scale at 1:50.

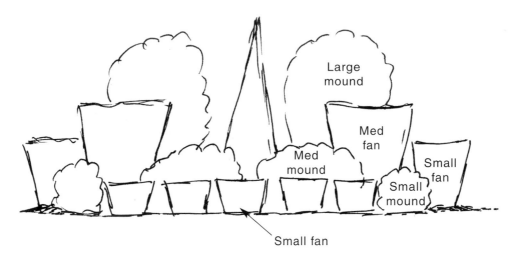

Planting scheme for dry, sunny, drawn with plant shapes.

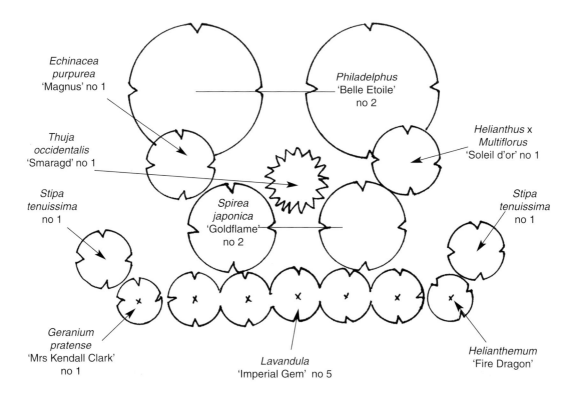

Planting scheme for dry, sunny, drawn as a planting plan, to scale at 1:50.

case, also improve the soil structure by 'bulking' it up as it decomposes and retaining moisture by reducing surface evaporation during the summer.

All of these measures will take time to show their effects, but the resultant healthy plants and thriving garden are well worth the effort. (Note that manure and tree bark should always be sourced from a supplier that guarantees that they have been stood for a minimum of twelve-months.)

Gravel garden

A gravel garden can be created whatever the aspect, whether sun or partial shade; it is simply the use of gravel as a mulch over Terram membrane that defines this type of garden. It is the most suitable garden type for the busy working couple with a family, or the elderly couple or single person who want to have an attractive garden with minimum maintenance.

A gravel garden is an area with a difference: the gravel surface, as well as being a mulch, also functions as a path but looks nothing like a path. A gravel garden can be developed as part of a garden, to create variety, or as an entire garden style.

As long as the plants are selected for the given soil type, the gravel garden will provide an attractive picture to be seen from the house, and require very little work to keep it looking good throughout the seasons and for many years to come. The plant selection will determine the style: it can be made to look modern and contemporary, more traditional, wildlife friendly, a permanent evergreen garden, or symbolic of a certain style, for example Italianate – the choices are wide and many.

In a gravel garden, and when used generally as a mulching material, the gravel is laid to approximately 50–75mm in depth on top of Terram membrane. Plant groups are situated throughout the gravel area; the users feel as though they are walking through a garden, with the gravel acting

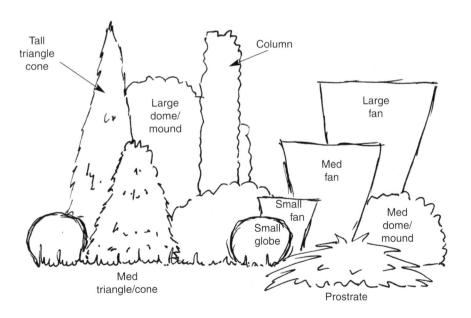

Gravel garden plant group drawn with plant shapes.

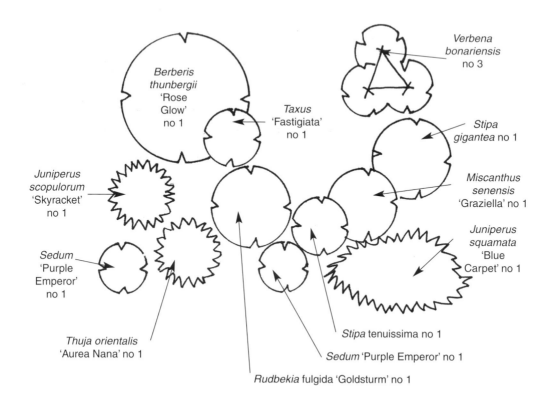

Berberis thunbergii 'Rose Glow' no 1

Verbena bonariensis no 3

Taxus 'Fastigiata' no 1

Stipa gigantea no 1

Juniperus scopulorum 'Skyracket' no 1

Miscanthus senensis 'Graziella' no 1

Juniperus squamata 'Blue Carpet' no 1

Sedum 'Purple Emperor' no 1

Thuja orientalis 'Aurea Nana' no 1

Stipa tenuissima no 1

Sedum 'Purple Emperor' no 1

Rudbekia fulgida 'Goldsturm' no 1

Gravel garden plant group drawn as planting plan format, to scale at 1:50.

A small plant group in gravel.

Gravel garden as viewed from the deck.

as a path, and the added bonus of no big borders to maintain. Any combination of plants can be used, as long as they are suitable for the given soil conditions.

There are many more growing permutations that the garden enthusiast and designer will come across, but they cannot possibly all be covered in this chapter. Those I have described demonstrate the role of the plant shapes method before the development of the planting plan format. The plant shapes stage should be sufficient for the garden enthusiast to determine the appropriate and most effective plant choice for the given growing environment. The planting plan stage provides a formal format for the professional designer, an additional stage which enables the designer to formulate not just a plant list, but a plant list with details of pot size and plant quantities required.

9 THE PLANTING PROJECT PROCESS

Form, harmony, contrast and balance combine to give a cohesive unit, in which every plant plays its part.

The planting phase of a garden project needs to be as carefully planned as the hard landscaping phase, in fact more so. This is the aspect of the project that brings the garden to life; the addition of the plants to the hard landscaping transforms the space into a living, breathing, evolving garden space. In order to avert any 'mistakes', complications or misunderstandings, it is necessary to follow a structured process that takes the designer and client through a series of stages in order to reach agreement upon all aspects of the final planting scheme, especially cost.

THE ROLE OF THE DESIGNER

There are three key skills that designers need to have at their disposal in order that this part of the project can run smoothly and result in happy clients and a beautiful garden. These are: knowledge of plants, spoken and visual communication skills, and organizational ability.

Plant knowledge

Designers need to know their plants in order to ensure that the selected plants are suitable for the given growing environment, the mature plants are still 'fit for purpose' in terms of their ultimate size, and the scheme provides seasonal interest – which of course is dependent upon a knowledge base of how and when each plant will perform within the scheme.

Communication skills

Communication skills, both spoken and visual, are essential primarily to ensure that the client understands the process, is kept fully informed at all times of progress and any changes, and as far as possible understands how the proposed planting is going to look. It is also key to the overall success of a project that the designer and contractor have a solid working relationship within which any changes to time-scale can be approached with a pragmatic 'What is the problem, what can be done about it?' approach. For the eventual success of the project, the designer's role is to act as a bridge between the client, the contractor and the suppliers, ensuring that all are made aware of any changes.

A planting sketch design meeting is the most effective method to ensure that a client understands the proposed scheme. At such a meeting the designer presents as many visuals as possible of the proposed scheme. These can be in the form of simple pencil sketches – the 'shapes method' is ideal for this – in conjunction with a digital image of each plant, shown on a PC or as pictures in books. A colour trace, overlaid on the planting areas, as per the design plan, is also a very effective method of demonstrating the proposed colour scheme.

The meeting is an ideal time to discuss with the client the estimated costs and its various components, such as any soil preparation that may be required prior to the planting; the estimated materials and labour, and whether or not tree bark mulch is to be applied. In this way, the client is fully informed as to all aspects of the planting phase and the individual components that make up the cost.

The process offers the client the opportunity to see the proposed scheme, to understand all aspects, and to discuss alternatives if they require any changes. The client is very much involved, giving them a sense of ownership.

The aim of the meeting is that it should conclude with an agreement on the costs and timescale of the proposed scheme, and that it can move forward from the planning stage to action, so that plants and labour can be organized.

Organizational ability

The success of the planting phase will largely depend upon the designer setting a logical series of events in motion.

Organizing a commencement date
This will depend upon contractor availability and plant supply, so clear communication needs to take place between the designer, contractor and suppliers. There should be a good working relationship in place between the contractor and designer. Then, in the event of delay because of overrun on a previous project, which may be due to circumstances beyond the control of the contractor, it can be discussed without bad feeling and an alternative date organized, agreeable to all.

Organizing, ordering and delivery of the plants
The plants should be delivered to the site on a date agreeable to all. The designer should be on site on the plant delivery day in order that a check can be made that all plants have been

supplied as specified and are of acceptable quality. If any substitutions have been made, the designer can accept or reject them as appropriate.

Setting out

This entails organizing the plants on site and is the role of the designer in order that last minute adjustments can be made. The planting plan is followed by the designer in terms of plant placement, but changes may be made when working with the living thing! If the designer is not on site the opportunity for these final adjustments is lost.

THE PLANTING PROJECT PROCESS

1. Cost estimate has been agreed and the final draft planting plan printed.
2. Check availability of plants and order from supplier. Payment in full for the plants may be required at this point, so it is perfectly acceptable to ask for a deposit from the client, to be deducted from the final invoice.
3. Order topsoil and tree bark if required.
4. Organize Day 1 of planting with contractors – if soil preparation needs to be carried out this may constitute the first day or two of the soft landscaping.
5. Organize delivery date, which could be Day 1 or otherwise of the planting phase, dependent upon whether any soil preparation is necessary – this can be agreed with the contractor, but it is preferable to get the plants on site earlier rather than later.
6. Planting work commences with 'setting out' – all the plants are set out, preferably by the designer, as per the planting plan.
7. Ensure that the root ball of each plant is well soaked prior to planting. If any root balls are pot-bound, tease the roots out at the base and around the sides before planting. The crown of the plant should sit just below the soil surface, or if a tree bark mulch is to be applied, just above the soil surface, in order that the plant crown is not swamped with tree bark, which could cause it to rot during the winter.
8. Finish with the application of tree bark mulch if required – this will need topping up every two to three years.
9. Walk the client around the garden and gain final approval for the work – some designers, as a personal choice, like to have this in writing. At this stage the maintenance requirements such as watering can be discussed; this will of course vary according to the time of year the planting has taken place. Long-term maintenance requirements can be discussed and agreed, depending on what level of service the independent designer can offer and the requirements of the scheme and client.
10. Organize a follow-up visit maybe four to six weeks later to check how the plants are settling in – if watering is not adequate or poorly done, this will be observed and can be flagged up with the client. Watering should always be to the base of the plants, rather than a light spray over the top.

This process is logical and works well in practice. By involving the client in the major decision-making stages and giving them a sense of being in control of the budget and the final scheme, major problems can be averted. This is a far better scenario than completing a planting job, presenting it to the client and finding they do not like it, or, worse still, presenting an invoice and they cannot pay it!

CONCLUSION

During the winter, our gardens may not be used for outdoor entertainment and activity or as an eating space, but they take on another role – a much more subtle role as the outdoor picture upon which we look to gain a sense of being re-energized and uplifted in these less inspiring months. The winter scene that we look out at can be just as beautiful: skeletal tree and shrub shapes covered in frost or snow; holly, cotoneaster and berberis with their adornment of bright red berries being pecked by feathered visitors during November and December; and in January and February the early, highly scented flowers on bare stems of *Sarcococca, Chimonanthus* and *Lonicera,* – all these are a strong reminder that new life is just around the corner. Confirmation of this comes as we eagerly watch the first snowdrop, iris and narcissus bulbs break through, bringing splashes of white, deep blue and bright yellow, their appearance telling us that a new year is beginning in the garden and in our lives, bringing renewed energy and hope for a year as good as, or better than, the last.

Our lives are intertwined with the seasons, in fact governed by them. Often, but not always, it is the purchase of a house with a garden in poor condition that is the trigger for the 'seed' of our garden interest to shoot and start growing. If this growth continues, it will provide physical activity, learning about nature and plants, and an opportunity to express our creativity through positioning and choosing plants for their individual characteristics of colour, season and shape.

When a project is completed, no matter how big or small, there is a great sense of satisfaction (most of the time anyway). And the more a project has been planned the better the result will be. In terms of planning the planting for an entire garden, or just a small area, bed, or border which needs rejuvenating, the plant shapes method provides a means of exploring the best options for creating a planting scheme that will, most importantly, be of great satisfaction and interest to us all year round.

Inevitably, the garden will change from year to year; as plants become larger their role will alter within the overall scheme. A small 45cm high shrub will eventually become a large 1.8–2m high shrub in approximately ten years, and its role then becomes that of a major plant in the scheme. This is where the plant shapes method and the time spent on plant research is essential, in order to maximize the possibility of the scheme working within such a time-scale. The great thing about gardens and plants is that as we look upon what we have created, if there is something 'not quite right' it can be changed – the plants can be moved to different places until it does look right. What looks right is very subjective, and will vary enormously from one person to another; again, this is where the plant shapes method provides a way for the proposed scheme to take on an increased, more meaningful form, transforming the plant list into a sketch in which the plants have height and depth – a visual form which is much easier to interpret.

Enjoy using the plant shapes method, explore it to the full, and a beautiful garden will be yours for the taking!

RECOMMENDED GARDENS AND NURSERIES

GARDENS

Abbotsbury Garden, Weymouth, Dorset
DT3 4LA
Tel: 01305 871387

The Bannut Garden, Bromyard, Herefordshire
WR6 5TA
Tel: 01885 482206

Beth Chatto Gardens, Colchester, Essex
CO7 7DB
Tel: 01206 822 007

Burford House, Tenbury Wells, Worcestershire
WR15 8HQ
Tel: 01584 810777

Compton Acres, Poole, Dorset BH13 7ES
Tel: 01202 700778

The Eden Project, St Austell, Cornwall
PL24 2SG
Tel: 01726 811911

Hampton Court Castle, Leominster,
Herefordshire HR6 0PN
Tel: 01586 797777

Kiftsgate Garden, Chipping Camden,
Gloucestershire GL55 6LW
Tel: 01386 438777

Knoll Gardens, Wimborne, Dorset BH21 7ND
Tel: 01202 873931

The Lost Gardens of Heligan, St Austell,
Cornwall PL26 6EN
Tel: 01726 845100

Mount Stewart Garden, County Down,
Northern Ireland BT24 7LH

Painswick Rococo Garden, Painswick,
Gloucestershire GL6 6TH
Tel: 01452 813204

Sezingcote Garden, Moreton-in-Marsh,
Gloucestershire GL54 9AW

RHS Rosemoor Garden, Devon EX38 8PH
Tel: 01805 624067

Westbury Court Garden, Westbury-on-Severn,
Gloucestershire GL14 1PD
Tel: 01452 760461

Winterbourne Botanic Garden, Edgbaston,
Birmingham B15 2RT
Tel: 0121 414 3832

NURSERIES

Badger Nurseries, Mappleborough Green,
Warwickshire
Tel: 01527 852631

Cotswold Garden Flowers, Badsey,
Worcestershire WR11 7EZ
Tel: 01386 833849

Knoll Garden Nurseries, Wimborne, Dorset
BH21 7ND
Tel: 01202 873931

Worlds End Nurseries, Hallow, Worcester
WR2 6NJ
Tel: 01905 640977

INDEX